The Forgotten Slave Trade

The Forgotten Slave Trade

The White European Slaves of Islam

Simon Webb

PEN & SWORD
HISTORY

AN IMPRINT OF PEN & SWORD BOOKS LTD.
YORKSHIRE – PHILADELPHIA

First published in Great Britain in 2020 by
Pen & Sword History
An imprint of
Pen & Sword Books Ltd
Yorkshire - Philadelphia

ISBN 978 1 52676 926 8

Printed and bound in England
By TJ Books Limited

Pen & Sword Books Ltd incorporates the Imprints of Pen & Sword Archaeology,
Atlas, Aviation, Battleground, Discovery, Family History, History, Maritime,
Military, Naval, Politics, Railways, Select, Transport, True Crime, Fiction,
Frontline Books, Leo Cooper, Praetorian Press, Seaforth Publishing,
Wharncliffe and White Owl.

For a complete list of Pen & Sword titles please contact

PEN & SWORD BOOKS LIMITED
47 Church Street, Barnsley, South Yorkshire, S70 2AS, England
E-mail: enquiries@pen-and-sword.co.uk
Website: www.pen-and-sword.co.uk

or

PEN AND SWORD BOOKS
1950 Lawrence Rd, Havertown, PA 19083, USA
E-mail: uspen-and-sword@casematepublishers.com
Website: www.penandswordbooks.com

MIX
Paper from
responsible sources
FSC
www.fsc.org FSC® C013056

Contents

List of Illustrations

1. The slave trade as most people understand it; black Africans transported across the Atlantic Ocean.
2. Christian slaves from Europe, on sale in a slave market in Algiers.
3. European slaves in North Africa at the end of the eighteenth century.
4. English slaves on sale in Rome in the sixth century.
5. The Hebrews as slaves in Ancient Egypt.
6. Black Africans being sold as slaves in nineteenth-century America.
7. Black African slave drivers, with African slaves.
8. A fierce Viking warrior.
9. Young boys from the Balkans being taken as slaves to Turkey.
10. Barbary corsairs approach a ship.
11. Lundy, a pirate island off the coast of Devon.
12. Some of the tortures to which Christian slaves in North Africa were supposedly put.
13. Jean le Vacher about to be blown from a cannon in Algiers.
14. The French bombardment of Algiers in 1688.
15. Kara Mustafa Pasha being strangled with a silk cord.
16. Thomas Jefferson, the man who dealt firmly with the Barbary corsairs.
17. Commodore Barron of the *Chesapeake* surrenders to officers of the Royal Navy.
18. British sailors battling Barbary corsairs.
19. The British bombardment of Algiers in the summer of 1816.
20. European slaves in Algiers in 1816.

Introduction

In recent years the subject of slavery has become quite literally a question of black and white. Upon hearing any mention of slavery, the mind of the average person in Britain or America turns unbidden, and as a matter of course, to the Atlantic slave trade, by means of which many black Africans were transported from their native continent to America and the islands of the Caribbean. For most of us, this is simply what slavery was; the historic mistreatment and exploitation of black people. It is widely accepted that anybody talking or writing about slavery must adopt this peculiar world-view and ensure that the central focus remains firmly upon black Africans. When we see a book in a library or bookshop called *The Slave Trade*, we have no doubt that when we open it, we shall be seeing graphic descriptions of the horrors of the so-called 'Middle Passage', which saw millions of men, women and children transported across the Atlantic Ocean in atrocious conditions. It is that grammatical feature, the definite article, which indicates what we are to expect. The word 'the' gives the game away. Illustration 1 shows the horrors of the transatlantic slave trade, an image familiar to us all.

To demonstrate the truth of the above proposition, it is necessary only to look at any book which claims to be about 'the' slave trade. *The Slave Trade* by Tom Monaghon, published by Evans Brother Ltd in 2002, is as good an example as any. As one would expect, looking inside reveals that just a single side of one page deals with the origins and history of slavery and that the rest of the book, with the exception of two pages at the end on modern slavery, is concerned solely with the Atlantic slave trade.

So prevalent is our horribly distorted perspective of this subject, the idea that the taking of black Africans across the Atlantic Ocean against their will was *the* slave trade, that the most trifling and inconsequential failure to abide by this modern convention is seen by many people as tantamount to heresy or, what is perhaps worse according to the *mores* of the Western World, racism. One or two specific examples should make this clearer, particularly if we examine them in depth and tease out all the implications. Doing so will serve also to introduce the main themes of this book.

Because many of those carrying out the dreadful traffic in human cargo which was the Atlantic slave trade were white, there now exists a general assumption that white people in Europe and America should have the grace to feel, at the very least, some vague sense of unease or possibly even guilt for the actions of distant ancestors who may have been connected, however tangentially, with the business. When the former Conservative minister Ann Widdecombe, in her maiden speech as a member of the European Parliament, compared the European Union to slave owners, the reaction was predictable and swift. She spoke of, 'oppressed people turning on their oppressors, slaves against their owners' (*Daily Telegraph*, 2019). It was, perhaps inevitably, taken for granted that Widdecombe had been referring to black slaves and their owners. She had said nothing of the sort of course; 'slaves turning against their owners' might easily have been referring to the slave rebellion led by Spartacus against Rome, but the assumption was that she had victims of the transatlantic slave trade in mind. Widdecombe was at once denounced for her insensitivity, her remarks were described as disgusting, and the general feeling was that a white person was appropriating the suffering of black people to make a political point and that this was, to say the least of it, in questionable taste. One man who was thoroughly affronted was the black British MP David Lammy, who said;

It is impossible to explain how offensive and ahistorical it is for you to equate my ancestors tearing off their chains with your small-minded nationalist project. Shame on you. (BBC, 2019)

It was clear by the mention of his ancestors tearing off their chains, that David Lammy had automatically taken Widdecombe's talk of slaves to be about black slavery. Because Lammy's parents came from the South American country of Guyana, he clearly felt that his family's past experiences were relevant to the case, they having been slaves, in sharp contrast to the forefathers of Ann Widdecombe, who came from the west of England. Since David Lammy apparently found it impossible to explain why he regarded Ann Widdecombe's talking about slavery to be so offensive, and because it is germane to the subject which we shall be exploring in this book, let us think a little about both his ancestry and that of Ann Widdecombe.

It is certainly likely that members of Lammy's family were slaves over 200 years ago, although Britain was hardly to blame for that. Guyana, or Dutch Guiana as it was between 1667 and 1814, was not ceded to the British until 1814, seven years after Britain abolished the slave trade. All the slaves in Guyana had been imported by the Dutch and none at all by the British. What about Ann Widdecombe? What are the chances that any of her own remote ancestors from centuries ago were slaves? This is an interesting point and reveals how little many people in Britain actually know about the history of their own country.

Ann Widdecombe was born in Somerset. Hers is what is sometimes termed a 'habitational' name, meaning that it is probably derived from a place name, somewhere that her family once lived. For those in Somerset, the most likely candidate for the origin of the Widdecombe name is the village of Wythycombe, which lies within the Exmoor National Park. In short, Ann Widdecombe's family probably have very ancient roots in that part of the West Country. Bath, where she was born, is just 12 miles from Bristol, a city which was, in the eighteenth century, a centre of the so-called 'triangular trade', the transport of slaves from West Africa to the Caribbean, the export of sugar and other cash crops from there to England and the carrying of manufactured goods from Britain to Africa. The well-known historian Asa Briggs stated bluntly that Bristol 'was the main English port involved in triangular trade' (Briggs, 1983). What is not commonly known is that Bristol's involvement with the trade in slaves pre-dates by almost a thousand years the period when it was renowned for its connection with the slave trade between Africa and the Caribbean. By the time of the Norman Conquest in 1066 Bristol was already an international centre for quite another kind of slave trade; that of exporting English slaves to Ireland and, from there, to Africa and Scandinavia.

Slavery was a well-established institution in Anglo-Saxon England and it continued to flourish even after the coming of the Normans. According to the Domesday Book, based on information collected in 1086, about a tenth of the English population were slaves (Trevelyn, 1942). Slaves were at that time acquired by traders across the whole of England and then transported to Bristol to be sold at the market there for export to other countries, principally Ireland (Rodgers, 2007). A contemporary writer described the scene at the Bristol slave market in the early eleventh century;

> You could see and sigh over rows of wretches bound together with ropes, young people of both sexes whose beautiful appearance and youthful innocence might move barbarians to pity, daily exposed to prostitution, daily offered for sale. (Pelteret, 2001)

Bristol was popular with slave traders because it was a handy English port from which to sail to Dublin. Dublin, Ireland's first town, was founded in 841 by Viking slavers (Haywood, 2008) and its prosperity and growth were closely bound up with the slave trade (Cunliffe *et al*, 2001). Some of the slaves brought to Dublin from Bristol were sold to buyers in Ireland, but others ended up in different parts of the world. It will perhaps come as a surprise to some modern readers to learn that English slaves sold in Dublin were at this time being bought by dealers who then took them to Africa (Haywood, 2008).

This is not the only possible risk which Ann Widdecombe's ancestors might have had of being captured and sold as slaves. Decades before England became involved in the African slave trade, which did not begin in earnest until after the English Civil War, slavers were raiding the West Country of England and carrying off the population of entire villages and taking them to be sold in African slave markets. In 1645, for instance, 240 men, women and children were seized when slave traders landed in Cornwall. These unfortunates were taken off to Africa. Illustration 2 is of a slave market in North Africa, of the kind where those seized in the raid on Cornwall ended up. Two years later, the island of Lundy, 12 miles from the coast of Devon, was occupied by slavers and on and off for the next five years and used as a base for their operations. Raids were made on coastal towns and villages by the men based at Lundy, who had arrived there from Africa. Illustration 3 is of eighteenth-century Europeans who have been captured by slavers and transported in chains to North Africa.

The lack of awareness of the slaving raids on England during the sixteenth and seventeenth centuries has been described by Professor Esra of the University of Exeter as 'cultural erasure' (*Daily Telegraph*, 2017). Although Professor Esra was referring specifically to the slave raids against Cornwall by ships sailing from Africa, this concept of cultural erasure applies more generally to the whole idea of slavery in the British Isles. At one time, the very concepts of 'Irishness' and 'Englishness' were inextricably bound up with the memory of the trade in English slaves. Dublin, the capital city of Ireland and iconic symbol of the Irish struggle for independence during the Easter Rising in 1916, was founded on the trade in English slaves, as too were Waterford and Limerick. The annual event of St Patrick's Day celebrates the life of a boy who was seized from his own country and carried off into captivity; St Patrick was of course an English slave. According to tradition Ireland's other patron saint, Saint Brigid of Kildare, was the daughter of a slave (Joyce, 1911). For the English, the association between their own national identity and the days when they were routinely carried off into slavery runs as deep as can be, because the idea of an 'English' nation began in a foreign slave market.

It was at one time a story known to every schoolchild in Britain. The Venerable Bede, an ecclesiastical historian of the Anglo-Saxon period, related how in the late sixth century Pope Gregory passed a market in Rome where he noticed some beautiful children for sale. On enquiring their nationality, he was told that they were Angles, meaning that they came from what is now England. He made a witty pun, saying 'Non Angli sed Angeli'; not Angles, but angels. It was after telling this anecdote that Bede began referring to the inhabitants of the southern part of Britain as 'English', the first recognition that the disparate collection of Saxons, Jutes and so on who had settled among the Romanised Britons might actually have a national identity of their own. This important historical incident may be seen in Illustration 4, as depicted in Westminster Cathedral.

Returning now to Ann Widdecombe and what David Lammy referred to as her 'ahistorical' remarks, it is clear that there is a good deal more to the case then is at first apparent. Ann Widdecombe had just as much right as David Lammy to talk about slaves turning against their owners, because her own ancestors almost certainly included slaves. The real question is why it should have been assumed in the first place that Widdecombe's comments about slave owners should have had anything at all to do with black slaves and how anybody could have been the slightest bit offended by them. We need to consider this strange state of affairs a little, otherwise it will be quite impossible to understand why the European experience of slavery has been almost entirely forgotten today. Part of the answer lies in the changing complexion of the European continent since the end of the Second World War. At that time, the nations of Europe were ethnically homogenous, which is to say that, with rare exceptions, only white people lived there. The altered demography of the twenty-first century, with waves of immigration from Africa and Asia, has caused us to treat with sensitivity, and attempt to share the perspective of, the various minorities who suffered under colonial systems and to try and see the world from their point of view, rather than merely our own. In the process though, a large chunk of the original history of the English, Irish, Spanish and Italian peoples has become obscured from sight or it has been felt that it is better overlooked or ignored.

The film *12 Years a Slave* was hugely popular at the box-office and it won three Oscars, including that for Best Picture. It tells the story, supposedly based upon the autobiography of the protagonist, of a free black man in New York who was kidnapped and then sold into slavery in the southern states of antebellum America. A film like *12 Years a Slave* fits neatly into our current cultural and historical framework. We know all about slavery in the United States and what a terrible thing is was. We are easily able to imagine a black man spending time as a slave in Louisiana and then after his release from captivity writing a book which reflected his experiences. What about a European man being kidnapped and sold into slavery in Africa though? This does not accord at all with our present-day notions about slavery and so is most unlikely to be made into an Oscar-winning film. How many readers even know that Miguel de Cervantes, author of *Don Quixote*, spent five years as a slave in Africa? A film about Cervantes' life called *Five Years a Slave* would just be confusing! How could one of the most famous European authors of all time have been a slave in Africa? It sounds ridiculous.

Mention of *12 Years a Slave* reminds us incidentally how little we really know about black people's experience of slavery. Almost all that we read about the subject has been written by white people and most of it has been exaggerated for various reasons, either to justify or condemn the practice. Of course, we know that the authors of books such as *Gone With the Wind* and *Uncle Tom's Cabin* were white, but the same applies to memoirs like *Twelve Years a Slave*. Although the film was allegedly based on the autobiography of a black man who had been enslaved, the book itself was actually written by a white man called David Wilson. Reading the book of *Twelve Years a Slave*, which we are led to believe gives us an insight into the actual life of a black slave, we find such gems as 'a shrewd, cunning negro, more intelligent than the generality of his race' (Northup, 1853). One can scarcely believe that a black man would really have written anything of this sort. Just as with *Gone With the Wind*, this book, ghost-written by a white man, tells us little about what black people actually thought about slavery or anything else.

Several forces are at play, which help to explain our almost total ignorance of any kind of slavery other than that suffered by black Africans. In Britain, one very obvious factor is that many white liberals feel a general guilt about the British Empire, colonialism and even the very colour of their own skins. This uneasiness about their own heritage has been caused, or at the very least exacerbated, by the large number of immigrants from what is sometimes called the 'New Commonwealth' who have settled in the United Kingdom since the 1960s. Guilt and angst about the legacy of colonialism and empire, of which the sight of black people and those of South Asian origin on the streets of the capital and other cities and towns are a constant reminder, can be assuaged in the most painless way imaginable by being enthusiastic about a film such as *12 Years a Slave* or taking part in campaigns to 'de-colonize' statues, buildings, cities or university curricula. Urging the removal of some Victorian statue or supporting a scheme to pay compensation to Caribbean countries for the suffering of their distant ancestors makes us feel both ethically virtuous and politically progressive. In the United States, guilt about the past treatment of African-Americans, not only during the days of the southern plantations but up to the institutional racism of the mid-twentieth century and later, serves the same function; to cause those white people with any pretension to being thought humane and liberal to keep constantly to the forefront of their minds the past suffering of black people, as exemplified by the slave trade. It hardly matters that both the scale and severity of this black slavery was far less than that of the white slavery at which we are going to be looking. The Atlantic slave trade is a handy talisman which, when brandished and wept over, shows that we are essentially right-thinking individuals.

This desire to purge themselves of the guilt felt for the actions of compatriots 200 years ago is particularly acute in British universities, several of which are now engaged in efforts to uncover any possible links with the eighteenth-century slave trade. In 2019 Bristol University appointed its first Professor of the History of Slavery. At first sight, this is quite an interesting idea. Bristol's history as a centre of the trade in slaves goes back over a thousand years and exploring it might well bring to light some new information relating to the relationship between England, Ireland, Scandinavia and North Africa. The hope that this newly-created post might involve a wider study of the institution of slavery than merely focusing on the 150 years or so that Britain was actively involved in the transatlantic slave trade was soon dashed, when the provost and deputy vice-chancellor of the University of Bristol, Judith Springer, announced that;

> This new role provides us with a unique and important opportunity to interrogate our history, working with staff, students and local communities to explore the university's historical links to slavery and to debate how we should best respond to our past in order to shape our future as an inclusive university community. (*The Independent*, 2019)

The university was not of course founded until 1909, a century after Britain's involvement with the slave trade ended, but it was clear that such a minor historical detail would not deter the project. The new professor herself, Olivette Otele, made it plain where her limited interests lay, when she said,

> I want students to see me as a facilitator of a dialogue that needs to take place and that is about the role of the University of Bristol in the transatlantic slave trade.

There was, apparently, no question of investigating slavery in general or even looking at Bristol's early role in the slave trade under the Anglo-Saxons. One cannot help but wonder if the University of Dublin has any plans to 'interrogate' its history on the subject of slavery. After all, Dublin's involvement in the slave trade dates back at least as far as Bristol's.

Apart from guilt about the British Empire and its role in the transatlantic slave trade, there is today another very powerful reason for wishing to expunge Britain's own experience of slavery from history and to pretend that it never happened. There are currently attempts to create a definition of 'Islamophobia' (*The Guardian*, 2019), it being undeniably true that there exists prejudice against Muslims in Britain. Almost all the slaves seized in Britain and the rest of Europe in the sixteenth and seventeenth centuries were captured by Muslims and were specifically targeted because they came from white, Christian countries. It is perhaps felt that such an unpalatable fact would be better overlooked or forgotten. Unfortunately, a side-effect of this sensitivity has from time to time unnecessarily tarnished the reputation of Britain and its empire, creating an altogether false view of the past.

The actions of the Barbary slave traders are more than merely an historical curiosity. They are the missing factor which enables us to make sense of much of the world's history, and understanding where this period of history fits in will enable us to understand both the present and the past more easily. From the origin of the British constitution to the tendency of the American armed forces to operate in the Middle East, the anxieties over immigration from Muslim countries to the savage wars which took place between the ethnic groups which went to make up the former country of Yugoslavia, an understanding of the struggle between Christian Europe and Muslim Africa and the Middle East is vital to properly make sense of the world in which we now live.

Before looking at the special kind of slavery which affected Europe and America from the sixteenth to nineteenth centuries, it might be best if we begin by examining the institution of slavery itself and seeing how it arose and why the religious restrictions place upon it by Islam had such a dramatic effect upon Christian nations.

Chapter 1

The Roots of Slavery

Fifty years ago, the idea that any discussion of slavery should be inextricably linked to the transportation of black Africans across the Atlantic to the New World would have struck most people as bizarre. Mention of slavery would, in the 1960s, have been as likely to evoke thoughts of Joseph being sold into slavery by his brothers or the ancient Israelites labouring in Egypt as it would the so-called 'triangular trade'. Illustration 5 shows the sort of scene which the word 'slavery' might have conjured up for a British schoolchild in the 1960s, with ancient Israelites in bondage before they were led across the Red Sea to freedom by Moses. Familiarity with the Bible was far more common in those days than now, and everybody knew about the stories of slavery found in the Old Testament.

That slavery had been widely practised in Britain in the past was also common knowledge at one time, although awareness of this has faded in recent decades. Glancing through books of popular history written and published in Britain before 1970 reveals many references to slavery in the country before the Norman Conquest, but these have tended to diminish with time. G.M. Trevelyan's *History of England*, published in 1942, contains ten references to slavery as practised in Britain. By the time that Kenneth Morgan's *The Oxford History of Britain* was published in 1984, slavery in the countries which make up the present-day United Kingdom is mentioned on only two pages. More modern books on the history of Britain omit the subject entirely and only mention slavery in the context of an institution inflicted upon black Africans. *British History for Dummies*, for instance, published in 2003, has quite a bit about Britain's involvement with the slave trade in Africa, but a single, brief mention of English slaves during the Iron Age (Lang, 2003). Reading such a modern book about the history of

Britain, nobody would guess that slavery was widely practised there during the thousand years of the Roman occupation and the Anglo-Saxon period.

Only a few years ago, the tale of Pope Gregory and his punning remark about the English slaves he saw in Rome, which we read about in the Introduction, would have been found in any children's history book published in Britain, usually accompanied by an illustration of the flaxen-headed children who roused him to pity. This, along with things such as David Livingstone's struggles against black slave traders in Africa, has been neatly erased and replaced by accounts of the cruelty of the wicked Englishmen who took part in the transatlantic slave trade.

All this is a clear illustration of the phenomenon of 'cultural erasure', which was also mentioned in the Introduction. For almost the whole of British history, slavery was a widespread and accepted part of ordinary life. As late as the Norman Conquest in 1066, a tenth of the people in England were slaves and even 600 years later, slavers were routinely raiding the shores of the British Isles. This aspect of the country's history has, in effect, been airbrushed away. A similar process has taken place in other European countries, where it is now felt tactful to avoid discussing slavery for fear of inflaming old divisions within the European Union and inciting racism against newcomers, many of whom are Muslim. It might help to set both the Atlantic slave trade and also the trade which saw Europeans being transported to Africa over the centuries in their proper perspective, if we look at the overall picture of slavery in history and examine its origins.

Some actions and activities have been universally condemned throughout the whole of recorded history. We know of no society where theft and murder by individuals were regarded as acceptable. In the same way, the cheating of customers by merchants has always been viewed as reprehensible. Telling lies and having sexual relations with somebody else's husband or wife have also been the subject of both legal prohibition and social disapproval throughout history. By contrast slavery, the ownership of human beings and their purchase and sale as though they were no more than domestic animals, has throughout almost the whole of history been seen as perfectly just and equitable and although restrictions have been placed upon the conditions of slavery, nobody until the last few centuries has seriously suggested that there might be something immoral or unethical about the idea of slavery in itself.

This is a strange state of affairs. Today, at least in the United Kingdom and the rest of Europe, most of us accept that a civilized society cannot tolerate murder, even that which is sanctioned and authorized by the state. We just know instinctively that it is wrong to kill people. We feel the same way about slavery. It is not necessary to advance arguments and delve into abstruse volumes on the subject of ethics for the average person to understand unreservedly that slavery, treating humans like cattle, is an abominable practice which must be supressed wherever it is found. So obvious does this seem that it is difficult to believe that the point of view is a relatively new one.

To understand the subject of this book, which is of course slavery, properly it will be necessary to bear in mind that across the world slavery has been an accepted and unremarkable institution for thousands of years. It has been widely practised throughout the whole of human history, right up to the present day. According to the United Nations, there are currently somewhere in the region of 25 million slaves in the world (*UN News*, 2019). It is notable that even in the earliest mentions of slavery, dating back 4,000 years, there is no suggestion of novelty about the practice, which indicates that by the time people began recording their history in permanent form, slavery was already a long–established tradition. It is clear that almost without exception, early civilizations regarded slavery as simply a convenient way of ordering societies which were, in the main, hierarchical. The emperor or king was at the top of the social order and slaves at the bottom. We search in vain for any condemnation of slavery in ancient writings. Even in the Bible and the Qur'an, slavery is regarded as an unremarkable part of ordinary life. There are certainly safeguards for slaves and recommendations for their humane treatment, but nobody seems to find the state of affairs whereby human beings are bought and sold as being in any way peculiar, let alone undesirable. There is no suggestion during the first 4,000 years of human history that slavery might actually be *wrong* (Everett, 1997).

The first reference to slavery of which we know dates back over 4,000 years. A century ago, a small, sun-baked clay tablet was excavated at Nippur, in what is today Iraq. It was a code of laws drawn up by the Sumerian king Ur–Nammu, who reigned from 2112 to 2095 BC (Cotterell, 1980). Slaves are mentioned several times and it is clear that they are regarded as chattels or belongings in just the same way as cattle and land. Three hundred years later, the Babylonian ruler Hammurabi promulgated a list of 282 laws, dealing, among other things, with the penalties for sheltering runaway slaves. Copies of these laws were ordered to be displayed in public places and a carved basalt column engraved with the laws is still in existence (Davison, 1992). These early codified laws are more than just historical curiosities. Hammurabi's laws probably provided the template, or at the very least the inspiration, for the regulations relating to slavery found in the Old Testament. One of the reasons for supposing this to be the case is that the Code of Hammurabi also includes the famous Biblical precept of an eye for an eye (Cotterell, 1980), which may also be found in the Book of Leviticus (Lev. 24:19–21). In both Hammurabi and the Bible, we find too the idea of the manumission of slaves after a certain number of years of servitude. According to the laws of Hammurabi, after three years a slave who was a fellow countryman should be freed. In Exodus, the second book of the Bible, the figure is set at six years for a Hebrew, following which he or she must be freed. None of this applied to foreign slaves, many of whom were prisoners of war and could be held indefinitely (Everett, 1997). This early mention of the different attitude to slaves who came from the same culture as the owner, as opposed to those who were foreigners, is a recurring theme which has particular relevance when we begin looking at the depredations of the Barbary corsairs, the slavers who plagued Britain for over a century.

It might seem incredible, but the principles set out in the Bible on slaves and their treatment, which date from the Bronze Age and were very similar to the laws of Hammurabi, were still being quoted and acted upon as late as the twentieth century, particularly in South Africa and the United States. Genesis, the first book of the Bible, contains a curious anecdote relating to Noah and his sons after the flood. After the waters had receded Noah planted a vineyard, following which he 'drank of the wine, and was drunken: and he was uncovered within his tent' (Genesis 9:21). One of his sons, Ham, saw his father naked and perhaps laughed at him. For this Noah cursed Ham's son Canaan, saying, 'Cursed be Canaan, a servant of servants shall he be to his brethren' (Genesis 9:25). This strange episode was embroidered and elaborated upon, until it seemed to make perfect sense for black men to be subservient to white people and even to be enslaved by them.

In Hebrew 'Ham' means 'hot' and it was deduced that Ham's descendants must be those living in the hottest part of the world, near the equator in Africa. This in turn meant that the black people living in that part of the world were, by Noah's curse as endorsed by God, destined to be servants and slaves. This flimsy rationale was used to support slavery in the southern states of America and later to justify keeping black people to menial jobs and a lowly position in American society (Whitford, 2009). As late as the 1960s, some American churches interpreted this verse of scripture to mean that the policy of segregating the races, with separate facilities for black and white, was divinely sanctioned. In South Africa the Dutch Reformed Church read in this part of the Book of Genesis God's encouragement for, and approval of, apartheid. This convoluted interpretation of scripture explains why slavery was so easily accepted in North America. Markets selling black slaves in America, such as that shown in Illustration 6, were justified because the word of God condemned Africans to being servants.

The ancient Hebrews both kept slaves of their own and were themselves enslaved. On occasion, the entire nation was reduced in status to that of slaves, first in Egypt and later in Babylon. Despite the laments about the subject, at no point in the Bible is the principle of slavery condemned. Even St Paul, that staunch evangelist for Christ's teaching, did not see anything wrong with humans being bought and sold. In his letter to the Ephesians, Paul said, 'Slaves, obey your human masters with fear and trembling' (Eph. 6:5).

Neither Judaism or Christianity viewed the institution of slavery as wicked or unjust, and although there were prohibitions on cruel behaviour towards slaves, the idea of treating human beings as objects to be owned is nowhere condemned. The same applies to the other great monotheistic religion of Islam. The Qur'an and the Hadith, a collection of stories about Mohammed which also details some of his teachings, both set strict limitations upon the practice, but there is no condemnation of slavery *qua* slavery. It is treated as just another unremarkable part of everyday life.

Slavery was a universal custom in the Middle East from the very earliest civilizations, which explains its ready acceptance in the major religions to arise in that region. The same was true of other parts of the world. In India, slavery was certainly common by the beginning of the Common Era and probably at the time of the Buddha, in the sixth century BC (Singh, 2009). There is reason to suppose that slavery was widespread in the earliest Chinese culture, the Shang dynasty, which flourished for about 700 years from the seventeenth century BC onward (Cotterell, 1980). In both India and China, as in the other civilizations at which we have looked, slaves tended to be drawn from nations or ethnic groups other than the one which was dominant. In other words, there existed a mild taboo on the enslavement of one's fellow countrymen, foreigners being preferred for the purpose.

On the other side of the world, in North and South America, the same general principle was followed, that captured enemies from other countries or cultural groups were seen as being natural candidates for slavery. The Maya followed this rule (Coe & Houston, 2015), as did the Aztecs and also the tribes of North America. In Alaska there lived two tribes who were very energetic and enthusiastic slave traders, whose raids extended all the way along the Pacific coast as far south as California. The Haida and Tlingit tribes both had fearsome reputations and routinely carried off men and women, taking them back to Alaska as slaves. The children of slaves also became slaves, unlike the situation in some American tribes, where children born to slaves might become full members of the tribe. As a result, in some parts of the North-West Pacific coast, a quarter of the population were slaves (McDonald, 1996). Long before the importation of African slaves to North America, slavery was flourishing among the indigenous inhabitants of the continent.

So widespread was the idea of enslaving prisoners of war and conquered peoples, among all cultures and historical periods, that it almost appears to be a natural law in the practice of slavery. It is also very noticeable that no religion seems to forbid slavery. Even those which hedge it around with restrictions and safeguards make it clear that there is nothing inherently offensive in the idea. These twin themes come together neatly in Islam.

The Qur'an, which is of course the holy book of Islam and had its origins in Arabia in the seventh century AD, both explicitly endorses slavery and at the same time imposes conditions upon its practice. The first of these limitations is one which we have already encountered, which is that only outsiders may be enslaved. This prohibition had serious implications, for it meant that when Muslim societies were hunting for slaves, they were compelled to look far afield, which explains why the raids on Europe took place. Much of the Qur'an is based upon the Bible and so it may be said that Muslim views on slavery are similar to, if not precisely identical with, those expressed in the Old Testament.

One reason that Muslims well into the twentieth century saw no objection to slavery, whatever anybody belonging to other cultures might think or say about it, was that the Qur'an is traditionally regarded as being God's own words, delivered to Mohammed by the angel Gabriel. Only the staunchest of Protestant fundamentalists would claim that the entire Bible consists solely of the Lord's words, with no human error having crept in over the millennia; in Islam, this is the orthodox and mainstream view. If the Qur'an accepts and endorses slavery, then this is God's view on the matter and there is no more to be said. This may go some way to explaining the differing perspectives on slavery found in Muslim countries as opposed to the rest of the world. Britain and America outlawed the slave trade over 200 years ago, but slavery was still legal in Saudi Arabia as late as 1961 and the Islamic Republic of Mauritania did not pass laws abolishing slavery until 1981.

Pre-Islamic Arabia was a bleak and desolate desert area. The major civilizations of Egypt, Assyria, Babylon, Sumer and Israel all arose in what is sometimes known as the 'fertile crescent', a vast swathe of land stretching in a broad curve from the head of the Persian Gulf, through modern-day Iraq and Syria and then down through Israel to Egypt. Arabia was not part of this area and was therefore something of a backwater during the first few thousand years of recorded history. It was to come to sudden prominence though in the seventh century, when the religion of Islam turned this neglected part of the world into a vigorous powerhouse.

Slavery was widely practised in Arabia before the arrival of Islam and it continued to be an important part of the economy despite the conversion of most of those living there to the new religion. The Qur'an is rather coy on the subject of slavery, using such euphemisms as 'those whom your right hand possesses' rather than referring outright to slaves. Nevertheless, it is obvious that slavery was not being abolished with the new religion, merely modified a little. We shall be looking in greater detail at the new perception of slavery which was introduced by Islam, but one point is especially notable. This is that, as in most other cultures at that time, a distinction was drawn between enslaving those belonging to one's own religion or ethnic group and making slaves of foreigners, particularly those captured during war. This was, as we have seen, a common enough rule in most ancient societies, but under Islam it was codified into detailed instructions about the correct treatment of, and methods of acquiring, slaves.

In this brief chapter we have seen that slavery is a custom which is found from the very beginning of recorded history. It appears to be a universal practice; the default setting, if you like, for civilizations. Because in the last couple of centuries slavery has been frowned on in some quarters and its abolition urged, it is easy to forget how widespread and accepted it was in almost every culture we study. The modern repugnance for slavery can lead us to take a jaundiced and distorted view of history. So terrible was the Atlantic slave trade that we might be tempted to regard is as a wicked aberration on the part of Europeans, rather than as part of a wider and more general pattern of world history in which all types of slavery fit without remark. This will be an important consideration when we look at the conditions of slavery under which white people were held in Africa and the Middle East, for the accusation might be made that examining those events is a way of minimizing the horrors of the triangular trade, about which most of us know. This is not at all the case. Rather, the intention is to put slavery in general into a proper historical context, one which will enable us to look dispassionately at the subject, without adopting a partisan attitude to this or that aspect of it.

We have glanced at slavery as it was practised in the Middle East and other parts of the world. Two large geographical areas were excluded from this survey; the continents of Africa and Europe. In the next chapter we will consider the situation in Europe, including Britain, up to the time that the Vikings came to prominence.

Chapter 2

Slavery in Europe until the
Coming of the Vikings

I n the last chapter we saw that slavery was a feature of almost all
ancient civilizations and that it was regarded as being more or less
the natural state of affairs in hierarchical societies, with the king
at the top of a triangle and slaves at the bottom. Slavery was every bit
as common in Europe in ancient times as it was in the Middle East.
Its absence in some specific part of the continent or other, for example
ancient Macedonia, is the object of remark because it is so atypical
(Cotterell, 1980).

There are two sources of information about slavery in Europe;
written accounts and archaeological evidence. References to slavery
in European inscriptions date back almost as far as those from the
Middle East. When the script of an archaic form of Greek called Linear
B was deciphered in the 1950s, it was found that frequent mention
was made of slaves. Most of the clay tablets recorded commercial
transactions and as well as sales of wine and grain, slaves were also
listed as commodities (Rodriguez, 1997). These lists were produced
around 1450 BC (Robinson, 2002). Beyond the bare fact that slavery
existed in the eastern Mediterranean at that time, these very early
records tell us little. Of far greater interest are texts such as the *Iliad*
and *Odyssey*. These epic poems were probably composed in the eighth
century BC, although incorporating material dating from the Trojan
War centuries earlier (Dudley, 1969). One must of course treat with
some little reservation a narrative in which gods often appear as leading
characters, but the fact that slavery was described in such a casual and
matter-of-fact way surely suggests that in Greece, almost a thousand
years before the start of the Common Era, the presence of slaves was

an accepted fact of life. As far as we can see, the relations between owners and slaves in Greece at that period were sometimes cordial and not in the least harsh. Eurycleia, Odysseus' old nurse from his childhood, speaks to him quite sharply at times, which suggests that although she was a slave she also regarded herself as being one of the family. Odysseus may have been the greatest hero of the Trojan War and a man of immense importance, but when he spoke to Eurycleia in a way that she considered impolite, she was swift to reprove him, saying, 'My child, no need to speak to me in that way!' (Homer, 1987). This may be fiction, but certainly suggests that whoever wrote it knew about the relations between slaves and their families in Greece at that time and depicted them in a way that his readers would not find too fanciful.

For the Greeks, slavery was almost an ideological matter. It may have been a practical necessity, to have free labour to undertake the less appealing tasks, but the philosophers of the time also saw the institution of slavery as a good thing in itself and the best way to order a civilized nation. The idealized society described by Plato in *The Republic* was supported by, and indeed founded upon, slavery (Plato, 2007). In other words, when an educated Athenian of the fifth century BC set out to devise a perfect state, he could not imagine it working well unless slaves were there to undertake the menial tasks. The reason was simple. The Greeks of that time believed that free citizens must be able to devote themselves to civil life and intellectual pursuits. Having to work too hard for a living might interfere with this lifestyle and so it was essential to have a good supply of slaves to carry out the monotonous and boring jobs.

It is impossible to say how many slaves there were in Greek city-states 2,500 years ago, at the time of Plato and Aristotle. One estimate is that in the peninsula of Attica, which includes Athens, there were in the fifth century BC around 100,000 slaves, perhaps a quarter of the population (Andrewes, 1971). In Sparta, free men were greatly outnumbered by the helots, who were a particular type of slave. Helots were the descendants of the original inhabitants of the territories of Laconia and Messenia, which had been occupied by the Spartans. According to the Greek historian Herodotus, the helots outnumbered the Spartans by seven to one. It is possible that this was an underestimate. We see again the same principle at work which we have already encountered, that slaves tended to be drawn from the ranks of outsiders; foreigners and those captured in battle. Useful though the helots were to the city-state of Sparta, they meant that the free citizens lived in a state of constant anxiety about the possibility of an uprising against them. For this reason, they treated the helots very harshly, humiliating them and every year holding a ritualized massacre of helots to remind them of their proper place in the order of things (Ducat, 1990).

So used are we to the subconscious association of the word 'slave' with the image of black people, that we might profitably pause at this point and remind ourselves that almost without exception the slaves in Europe were all white. The evidence for this is conclusive. In Greece, for example, there are many paintings on vases and dishes of slaves going about their work and they are all clearly white Europeans. A few Africans were imported via the Upper Nile, but these were by way of being novelty items. There is a tiny and perfectly modelled figure of a black slave boy, sleeping against the amphora which he had apparently been carrying. A number of jugs and vases also bear images of black people, but there is no archaeological evidence to suggest that these Africans were anything other than oddities. Almost without exception, the slaves shown in visual images are white people, ethnically indistinguishable from their masters and mistresses. In Roman society too, almost all of the many millions of slaves came from those parts of the continent which are today Germany, France and Scandinavia and hardly any at all from Africa.

How do we know the ethnic composition of Ancient Rome? The answer is that between a third and four-tenths of the city's population were slaves and they tended to be buried without elaborate tombs, grave goods or even markers. Excavating an ordinary cemetery will almost certainly mean encountering a large proportion of burials of slaves. In recent years, a number of large-scale surveys of burial grounds from the days of Imperial Rome have been undertaken and the bones analysed for various trace elements and so on which enable us to be fairly sure which part of the world the person came from. Water from different sources causes isotypes of oxygen to build up in varying levels in tooth enamel, meaning that it is possible to be fairly sure where an individual spent his or her childhood. One such examination of the necropolis of Isola Sacra, near Rome, found that many of those buried there had been born and spent their childhoods in other parts of Europe, which suggested that they may have been slaves captured and brought to Rome. Of the sixty-one bodies examined, only one had elements in the bones consistent with an origin outside Europe, namely North Africa (Prowse *et al*, 2007). Slavery in Europe was at that time almost exclusively a European affair.

A century or so after Homer composed his epic poems, a vigorous group of tribes in central Europe began to expand outwards in all directions (Haywood, 2008). Physically, the migration of the Celts took them south into Italy and west towards the English Channel, but their cultural influence extended a good deal further, from the regions which are now Turkey and the Ukraine as far as the Atlantic coast of Ireland. Among the cultural traditions of the Celts were the language which they spoke, distinctive artistic styles of metalwork and of course slavery. That slavery was an important part of Celtic life is shown by the fact that long after the rest of Europe had abandoned slavery, it lingered on, along with the Celtic language, in that part of Europe which became known as the Celtic Fringe, which consisted essentially of Ireland, Wales, western Scotland and Cornwall. Slavery still flourished in those places in the Middle Ages and it took the Norman Conquest to put an end to it. As with other nations and ethnic groups, slaves were usually captives seized from territory which had been attacked or invaded.

It was in the Roman Empire that slavery reached such vast numbers as to dwarf the Atlantic slave trade and allow us to see it in its proper perspective. In the early years of the Roman Empire there were perhaps 10,000,000 slaves at any one time, which was between one–fifth and one-sixth of the entire population (D'Arms & Kopf, 1980). The same source suggests that more than half a million new slaves would have been needed every single year. If these numbers are accurate, and they are taken from the proceedings from an academic conference on Roman commerce, then the implications are startling. In the city of Rome alone, there were, during the reign of Trajan, an estimated 400,000 slaves, a third of the city's population (Davison, 1992).

A quick calculation reveals something which may come as a shock to many readers. It has been estimated that in the three and a half centuries after Columbus first reached the Caribbean, between 8,000,000 and 11,500,000 black slaves were transported across the Atlantic Ocean before the end of this particular trade (Everett, 1997). This figure is sometimes adduced as evidence of the uniquely awful nature of the triangular trade; over 10,000,000 people snatched from their homes and carried off into involuntary servitude. Let us now compare this with the situation at the time of the Roman Empire. The life expectancy of a slave in the Roman Empire was quite astonishingly low. Males could expect, on average, to live to the age of 17.2 years and females 17.9 (Harper, 1972). By way of comparison, the life expectancy of a slave on an American plantation in 1850 was 36 (Fogel & Engerman, 1974). Because life expectancy for Roman slaves was so low, it meant that the only way that a constant population could be maintained was not by relying upon natural increase, but rather by constantly seizing new land and capturing those living there. For this reason, it has been suggested that around half a million new slaves would need to have been seized every year (D'Arms & Kopf, 1980). This would amount to 12,500,000 people in just 25 years. The figure for the slaves transported in the course of the Atlantic slave trade indicate that this number were taken from Africa to the Americas and the Caribbean in 350 years. In short, the Roman slave trade in Europe and the Middle East was probably more than ten times as extensive as that which was carried out across the Atlantic, between Africa and the New World.

The idea that the Atlantic slave trade might not have been the greatest or worst trafficking in slaves of which we know is a novel one for most people. Certainly, for a generation which has been raised on horror stories of what has come to be known as *the* slave trade, it will come as a shock to discover that there was nothing to distinguish that slave trade from any other. Neither the numbers involved nor the treatment of the slaves is remarkable when considered in a wider historical context. Some European slaves were certainly treated more leniently than those in America and the Caribbean, but many were also kept under far harsher and more punitive conditions.

In Britain, both archaeological evidence and written sources attest that slavery existed during the Iron Age and probably much earlier. The Greek geographer Strabo, writing in about AD 10, described Britain in these terms, 'It bears grain, cattle, gold, silver, and iron. These things, accordingly, are exported from the island, as also hides, and slaves, and dogs that are by nature suited to the purposes of the chase' (Strabo, 1923). It was noted above that in Britain at that time, the Celtic language was spoken and the customs of the Celts followed. Trading in slaves was therefore a quite normal commercial undertaking. A century or two before Julius Caesar landed in Britain in 55 BC, tribes from what is now Belgium and France established themselves in southern Britain. Assuming that the same general rules were followed as in the rest of the historical record, those who were already living in the country would have been seen as fair targets for slavers, not belonging to the invading tribes. It was most likely they who were being exported to mainland Europe.

We do not need to take Strabo's word for the presence of slavery in Britain before the Roman invasion. There is more tangible proof. A number of iron 'gang chains' have been unearthed in Britain and they date back some 2,300 years. One of particular interest was found in Wales (Williams, 2006). During the Second World War in 1942, the RAF were constructing a new runway on the Welsh island of Anglesey. An old iron chain was dredged from a small lake called Llyn Cerrig Bach. It was in such remarkably good condition that the men working on the runway used the used the chain about the base, attaching it to a tractor to pull out cars which were stuck in the mud at the edge of the lake.

In fact, the iron chain was over 2,000 years old and had been used to link together five people by means of metal collars which fitted around their necks. It is very similar to chains used in other places to control a group of slaves and prevent any of them slipping away when their guard's back is turned. At Bigbury Camp, near Canterbury, another set of iron chains were excavated. These were leg shackles, long enough to enable a slave to shuffle from one place to another, but short enough to prevent any running or even striding briskly. The discovery of these chains ties in with Strabo's assertion that slaves were exported to Europe. Whether they were sold to Celts or Romans is an open question.

There is also plenty of similar evidence to show that slavery was a popular system once the Romans occupied Britain from AD 43 onwards. We know that the Roman Empire was heavily reliant upon slavery and there is no reason to suppose that Britain would be different from the rest of the empire. From Roman authors, we know that the shackling of slaves was common and in addition to the Celtic chains found in the country, there are also others of obviously Roman manufacture. Near Winchester, in the English county of Hampshire, Roman shackles have been unearthed and in Norfolk, shackles attached to a bar with an integral padlock. These would have made it all but impossible for the person locked into them to walk more than a few paces. Sometimes, shackles were permanently attached to Roman slaves. In an archaeological dig at Saintes, in France, a cemetery was excavated in 2014 and some of the bodies were found to have been buried with the iron rings still around their necks and legs. Saddest of all was a child who had died and been buried with a metal ring around his wrist (*Daily Mail*, 2014).

Some British slaves would have worked in their own country, while others would have been sent to whichever part of the empire could best benefit from their labour. These were, after all, merely possessions of their owners. They had no more say in where they lived and worked than a horse or dog would have.

Further archaeological evidence for slavery in Britain during the Roman occupation is provided by finds of miniature figures depicting bound captives. These are people shown with ropes around their neck, which are connected to their hands and feet, which are also bound. Twelve such figurines have been unearthed in Britain, all dating from the second or third century AD. Their purpose is obscure. All the known examples, both from this country and the frontier of the Roman Empire, along the line of the Rhine and Danube, have holes at the back so that they could be mounted in some way.

Slavery existed in Britain before the coming of the Romans and it certainly lingered on after they left in the fifth century AD. The Celts both traded in slaves and kept them for their own personal use, and so did the Romans. The Angles, Saxons and Jutes who arrived after the legions were withdrawn also approved of slavery and practised it after their arrival in England. When they in turn were displaced by Vikings, slavery continued. All the evidence suggests that slavery was a feature of British life from the earliest times until some decades after the Norman Invasion in 1066. During most of that time, slaves were traded to and from the Continent, being taken across the English Channel by boat. Some found their way as far as Rome, but almost without exception, British slaves remained in Europe. It was not until the coming of the Vikings, some centuries after the Romans left, that slaves from Britain began to be taken further afield, to Africa and the Middle East.

Slavery was a well-established custom throughout the whole of Europe from the earliest times. The slaves were, almost without exception, European and when they were bought, sold or transported from place to place, they remained in Europe. This situation changed dramatically in the seventh and eighth centuries AD, when the Vikings began spreading out from their ancestral homelands in Scandinavia. The Vikings not only kept domestic slaves for their own use, but traded them to the rest of the world as valuable commodities. It was at this time that white slaves from Europe began to be sold to buyers in Africa.

In keeping with the common practice which we have observed from the earliest records of slavery, the Vikings preferred to enslave and sell those from cultures other than their own. As they began to explore the world and loot it of whatever riches took their fancy, it was not perhaps surprising that they came to be aware of the potential profits to be made from seizing captives from one country and then selling them to another.

Chapter 3

Exporting Concubines and Eunuchs from Europe to Africa

From time to time during the days of Greek and Roman dominance of the Mediterranean and the lands surrounding it, black slaves from Africa were brought to Europe. This was not a common occurrence, and when skeletons of apparently African origin are found, they are acknowledged to be rarities (Prowse *et al*, 2007). There is a paucity of other evidence for extensive contact between Europe and Africa, beyond a few Greek vases and the occasional painting or figurine. The traffic in slaves between the two continents did not begin in earnest until the seventh or eighth century AD and when it did the traffic was in the opposite direction to that which most people would suppose. Rather than African slaves being brought to Europe, it was white Europeans who were taken to Africa to be sold in slave markets. To see why this should have been, it will be necessary to look in some detail at the history of Africa.

When thinking of Africa, we must never forget that it is a vast continent, as varied and diverse in ethnicity, language and culture as Europe. About 2,500 BC, sub-Saharan Africa consisted of three main ethnic groups. These were the Bantu of what is today Nigeria and Cameroon, the 'pygmies' of the East African rain forests and the Khoi people in the south, who are sometimes known as 'bushmen'. The Khoi, who are limited today to a few small areas of the Kalahari Desert, have the most ancient lineage of any group of people in the world. They are, if you like, the original humans (Haywood, 2008).

For reasons which we are never likely to know, connected perhaps with the changing climate at that time, the Bantu-speaking tribes from West Africa began to spread out from their homelands and moved east and south as they effectively colonized the rest of Africa. This migration began in 2,500 BC and continued for about 3,500 years. The Bantu were farmers and pioneers in ironworking. The story of their languages and culture spreading across an entire continent is similar in many ways to that of the Indo-Europeans, who, a thousand years earlier, had begun their own migrations into India and Europe. A more sophisticated society which practises agriculture will, almost as a matter of course, tend to displace groups of hunter-gatherers. So it was that as the centuries passed, the pygmies and the Khoi were pushed from their own lands by the Bantu and often enslaved in the process.

While on the subject of slavery in Africa, it is worth remembering that although Europeans and Americans are today wringing their hands and agonizing over the treatment of black African slaves a century or two ago, there are still plenty of black slaves to be found in the world, most of them in Africa itself. In the Republic of Congo, one of the areas conquered by the Bantu, many of the Pygmies who are the descendants of the indigenous inhabitants are still slaves. The ruling Bantus describe this arrangement as a 'time-honoured tradition' (*News & Observer*, 2007). Pygmies make up between 5 and 10 per cent of the 3.7 million people living in the Congo.

One thing which must be borne in mind is that just as Europe and the Middle East had a strong tradition of slavery, based frequently upon the capture and exploitation of prisoners of war, so too did a similar process take place as the Bantu conquered Africa. By the time that European explorers and colonizers arrived in Africa, slavery was an accepted way of life across most of the continent. It made perfect sense for African kingdoms to do business with the newcomers, trading slaves which they acquired from neighbouring territories and exchanging them for firearms and manufactured goods.

The history of slavery in Africa is a fascinating study in itself, for it was as firmly rooted in that continent as anywhere else in the world. Even when the British themselves renounced slavery at the beginning of the nineteenth century, many Africans were determined to continue both keeping and trading slaves. The buying and selling of slaves took place sometimes between different tribes and also with the Arabs who catered for the demand for slaves in places like Zanzibar. It is easy to forget just how established slavery was in all parts of Africa and how it proved impossible to stamp out, despite the best efforts of the British administrators. In some territories which were nominally under British control, Sierra Leone for instance, slavery was widely practised in the interior as late as 1928 and largely tolerated by the British as the natives seemed so reluctant to abandon the custom (Miers & Kopytoff, 1977).

We have already observed that 50 or 60 years ago, nobody in Britain would have thought of the transatlantic slave trade as being *the* slave trade. It was rather thought of, quite correctly, as one of many. Children in the 1960s grew up with a broader awareness of the history of this topic than is perhaps the case today. The only references to slavery that the average schoolchild in the United Kingdom is likely now to encounter relate to the iniquities of the triangular trade, the teaching about which is a recommended, although not compulsory, part of the National Curriculum. In practice, every school in the country covers this topic and during Black History Month in October, pupils receive a top-up, to remind them about this type of slavery and ensure that they understand its importance.

To see how a previous generation of children, those whom we now refer to as 'Baby Boomers', might have become acquainted with slavery in Africa, we look at a children's non-fiction book published in 1960. The Ladybird books in the 'Adventures from History' series were enormously popular and found in every library and school, as well as many private homes. They were written by Lawrence du Garde Peach. The one which he wrote about David Livingstone shows perfectly what children would once have been reading about slavery in Africa. The account is of Livingstone's encounter with slave traders;

> What was known as 'the slave trade' was being carried on all over this part of Africa. Men, women and children were captured by fierce savages, and then sold as slaves. Livingstone determined to do what he could to stop this terrible state of things. (Peach, 1960)

The illustrations, and also further references to slaves and slave trading, make it quite clear that what is meant here by 'the slave trade' is black Africans enslaving other Africans. This is interesting, as it shows how the expression has, over the last few decades, been appropriated by those who are determined that white people alone should feel guilt for the practice of trading in slaves. On another page, there is a lurid picture of Livingstone and his black servants driving off an attack by a body of black warriors. The text explains;

> The savage slave raiders were not long in trying to revenge themselves on Livingstone for having freed the slaves. One day, when he was travelling with a party of missionaries who had come out from England, they were suddenly attacked by the Ajawas.

Things like the Ladybird book which is quoted above, together with a greater familiarity with Old Testament bible stories than is now common, meant that those growing up in the 1960s had no narrow view of what constituted slavery or the slave trade. From David Livingstone's experiences in the nineteenth century to the selling of the Old Testament character Joseph into slavery by his brothers, slavery was understood to be an ancient custom, practised across the world at different times, that had now fallen into disuse. We see in Illustration 7 some black African slaves and the Africans who have captured them to sell on to others.

We shall touch in a later chapter on the Arab slave trade in East Africa, which continued for many years. For now though, we turn to the situation in North Africa which was rather different, although there too slavery was a way of life. In the lands fringing the Mediterranean lived the Berbers. As far as can be ascertained, the Berbers are the original inhabitants of this part of Africa. The name 'Berber' is a variation of the Greek word 'barbaros', from which we get the modern expression 'barbarian'. It was applied by both the Greeks and Romans to peoples or tribes whom they regarded as being uncivilized. The people of North Africa have been known as Berbers for at least 2,000 years (Schoff, 1912).

In the seventh century AD, the newly-created Arab religion of Islam began to be forcibly spread to the countries contiguous to Arabia, the area roughly equivalent to modern-day Saudi Arabia. Mesopotamia, Syria and Egypt adopted the new faith and it was also carried west, along the Mediterranean coast to the Berber tribes which occupied what are today Algeria, Tunisia, Morocco and Libya. Between the years 642 and 708, Arab armies conquered the whole of North Africa from Egypt to the Atlantic Ocean and imposed Islam upon the region. The Berbers were crushed and most converted to Islam. In the course of the 70 years or so which it had taken to subdue this vast area, hundreds of thousands of slaves had been acquired. These were those defeated by the Arab armies (Pipes, 1981). It was at this time that a subtle shift took place in the nature of slavery, at least in Europe, North Africa and the Middle East.

Until the rise of Islam and the contemporaneous Arab conquests, there was a tacit understanding across most of the Europe and the Middle East that while it was quite all right to make slaves of those belonging to other nations, it was not really the thing to enslave one's fellow countrymen. This distinction was observed in most cultures. With the coming of Islam, nationality was no longer the crucial point, but rather religious faith. Mohammed, the founder of Islam, was not initially opposed to the keeping of slaves. He bought and sold slaves himself. What he set out in the Qur'an were new rules for the treatment of slaves. They were to be regarded as fellow human beings, rather than just possessions, and freeing them was presented as a charitable and meritorious act. In the Hadith, more restrictions on the practice of slavery are to be found. For the devout Muslim, only two ways of acquiring slaves were now acceptable. One of these was if a child was born into slavery, the offspring of two slaves. The other was by capturing people in the course of war, which was of course already at that time a long-established method of creating new slaves. There was though a new limitation on this practice too.

Traditionally, soldiers and civilians belonging to an enemy nation could be seized and enslaved when their territory had been overrun. It did not matter which gods, if any, they worshipped; the important thing was that they belonged to another nationality or ethnicity. For Islam, the case was now altered, for it was forbidden to enslave any free Muslim. It did not matter if the person was black or white, Arab or Berber, rich or poor; Muslims could not be made slaves. This meant of course that if a steady supply of new slaves was required, it would be necessary either to keep fighting wars of expansion against non-Muslim countries or to resort to buying them from slave traders. This was frowned upon, from a strictly religious viewpoint, but just about tolerated as long as the slaves being bought were not Muslims.

As we shall see, this new idea of a prohibition on the acquisition of slaves based not on nationality but rather on religion, had a profound influence on slavery from the seventh century onwards. Precisely similar prohibitions were also placed upon Christians in later times, in that only non-Christians could be captured as slaves.

The conquest of North Africa had yielded up to 300,000 slaves and the rapid growth of Islam in the wake of the invasions may have owed at least as much to the desire of the conquered Berbers not to end up as slaves as it did to the merits of Islam as a religion. The only test of whether somebody was really a Muslim was a simple one. If they were able to declare, 'There is no God but Allah, and Mohammed is his messenger', then that person was a Muslim. This simple statement of faith alone was sufficient to prevent anybody in Muslim-dominated territory being seized and taken into slavery. There was an added bonus to being a Muslim, in that Muslims were taxed more lightly than Christians, Jews or out-and-out heathens.

From Africa, the Muslim expansion continued across the Straits of Gibraltar and into the Iberian Peninsula. By 715, the whole of Spain was in Muslim hands and the following year, the Portuguese city of Lisbon fell. Having gained a foothold in Europe, the time seemed ripe to ride north, just as the Muslim hosts had swept east and west, encountering no opposition which could not be brushed aside in short and bloody wars. In 720, a huge army of 90,000 Arabs crossed the Pyrenees and entered France (Castleden, 2005). Over the next few years, the invading Arabs occupied a number of cities and thrust into the heart of the country. Then, in 732, they were halted at Poitiers and defeated by a Christian army. It was a turning point in world history, because it prevented Europe becoming Muslim as so many other parts of the world had done at that time. The Middle East, North Africa, Persia, Afghanistan; all have remained Muslim to this very day. The Battle of Poitiers though meant that Europe was, in the main, destined to be Christian.

The Muslim world of the eighth century thus covered a very great area, and most of those living in countries such as Syria, Egypt and so on professed to be Muslims. A word needs to be said at this point about the mode of government of such a vast empire. After the death of Mohammed in 632, a successor was chosen, a man who would be both the religious and civil leader of the expanding Muslim empire. This person would have spiritual and temporal authority and his role might, very roughly, be compared to that of the Pope in the Catholic Church. These successors were known as caliphs and they wielded an extraordinary amount of power. The first caliphs were related to Mohammed, either by marriage or blood (Kennedy, 2016).

The idea that slaves could only be non-Muslims from outside the empire created something of a dilemma, because it meant that they would in future need to be acquired from the beyond the borders of the Muslim lands. It was a question of looking south or north. One way of getting them would be to launch raids against non-Muslim countries and simply carry off men and women by main force. This was regularly done in both Europe and Africa. The other way to get slaves would be to buy them, just as one would do with any other desired commodity. It is perhaps no coincidence that it was at this time that the Vikings from Scandinavia began to engage in the slave trade. We often tend to think of the Vikings as ferocious pirates who sacked monasteries and pillaged wherever they were able, but there was invariably a strong business-end to their activities and when they found that there was a good market for living captives, rather than dead victims, they eased up on the slaughter and began taking prisoners instead and selling them to the Muslim world.

The Vikings burst onto the historical record in the summer of 793, when a raid was carried out on the monastery of Lindisfarne, off the coast of northern England (Parker, 2014). Many of the ecclesiastical articles at Lindisfarne, the candlesticks, containers for the host, boxes containing holy relics and so on, were made of silver and gold. Some monks who tried to protect what they thought to be sacred objects were killed out of hand. This tended to be the pattern for a few years, until the Vikings, who came from Scandinavia, the northernmost part of Europe, realized that young monks and nuns were in many ways even more valuable than the precious metals which they were stealing. A century after that first raid on Lindisfarne, a Flemish monk called Rimbert was visiting the Viking trading centre of Hedeby, in modern-day Denmark. He was horrified to find a nun who had been taken prisoner and was being sold as a slave. Rimbert managed to raise enough money to free the unfortunate woman. By this time, in the late ninth and early tenth century AD, the Vikings had found that the most profitable market for slaves, especially those who were young and attractive, was the Muslim world, both North Africa and the Middle East. Illustration 8 shows the popular idea of a Viking warrior; a fierce marauder stepping from his ship to carry out acts of pillage and rape.

Apart from general slaves who would be labourers, domestic servants and so on, three specific kinds of slave were in great demand by Muslims. These were attractive young women, strong, healthy adolescent boys and eunuchs. The next chapter will deal exclusively with the desire of various caliphs to have a steady supply of young men who were not Muslims to train as elite troops. For now, we shall be looking at the demand for women and eunuchs.

Polygamy is not forbidden in Islam. Mohammed himself had a dozen wives (Armstrong, 2006) and some of his later followers had many more than this, as well as large numbers of concubines. The maintenance of a harem consisting of many wives and sex-slaves was a sign of wealth and importance in Muslim society for some centuries. It must be borne in mind that neither the Christian nor Hebrew Bibles forbid polygamy and that some of the most revered figures in both religions practised polygamy to such an extent as to make Mohammed and his successors seem positively restrained in their appetites! King Solomon, for example, was said to have 700 wives and 300 concubines (1 Kings 11:3). Even the most famous of the sultans does not come near to matching this incredible harem.

The word concubine may be familiar to most readers, although its precise meaning obscure. The status of concubines varies greatly between cultures and historical ages. Concubines are women who have a regular sexual relationship with a man and yet are not married to him. Sometimes, concubines are indistinguishable from mistresses, in that they are not married and their children are illegitimate. In other cases, the concubine is very similar to a wife, although one of slightly inferior standing. In Islam, concubinage was an accepted institution and rich and powerful men wanted to have as many concubines as they could afford to keep. To keep a harem was a display of ostentatious wealth. It meant that in addition to wives, the owner of the harem could have his pick of other attractive women who were bound to allow him sexual access to their bodies. Many of these women had been purchased as slaves.

To guard and protect their harems, important and powerful Muslims required eunuchs; men who were incapable of taking surreptitious advantage of all those attractive women. Eunuchs were men who had been castrated, so that they were no longer able to perform sexually. There was a problem with finding eunuchs though, because the Hadith contained the express and precise views of Mohammed on the whole idea of castrating or otherwise harming slaves. His opinion on the matter could not have been plainer: 'Whoever kills his slave, we will kill him: whoever mutilates [his slave], we will mutilate him, and whoever castrates [his slave], we will castrate him' (Sunan an-Nasa'i 4736).

This all seemed quite straightforward; a devout Muslim was not able to castrate one of his slaves. There was incidentally another and more practical reason not to try and create eunuchs and this was that the death rate among grown men who were castrated was very high, either from infection or post-operation complications such as the urethra becoming blocked and the victim's bladder bursting as a result. One estimate was that for men past puberty, the mortality rate could be as high as 90 per cent. Even when the procedure was carried out skilfully by those well practised in it, the majority of those subjected to this hideous operation, carried out without anaesthetics, did not survive. In the sixteenth century, many eunuchs were created at a Coptic monastery in Egypt. Despite taking every precaution and being very skilled at the operation, two-thirds of those castrated at this monastery died (Wilson & Roehrborn, 1999). This, remember, was under the best possible conditions for the time.

The solution to the difficulties, both practical and religious, which prevented Muslims from making their own eunuchs was to engage slave traders in Europe to provide a ready-made product which could then be purchased, already castrated and in good health. These eunuchs were manufactured in Europe, from pre-pubescent European boys and the history of the vile trade has almost been forgotten today.

Whatever other horrors the Atlantic slave trade entailed, routine castration was never one of them. It is true that black slaves in America and the Caribbean were from time to time castrated, but this was never a common occurrence and was usually inflicted due to exceptional circumstances, such as an accusation of rape. With the act of castration so likely to result in death, it would have made no sense to hazard the lives of slaves in this way too frequently. In Europe, by contrast, the castration of white slaves was carried out on an industrial scale (Tracy, 2013). In Venice and the French city of Verdun 'castration houses' were set up to produce eunuchs for export to Egypt and other Muslim countries. The majority of the young boys were Slavs taken prisoner by the Vikings and then sold on to slavers. The Slavs, from whose name is derived the modern word 'slave', are an ethnic group which originated in what is today western Russia. By the sixth or seventh century AD, they had spread south into the Balkans, almost as far as Greece, and west into what is now Poland.

Before we look at the trade in, and creation of, eunuchs, it might be interesting to think a little about the mechanics of the thing and why there were such difficulties in maintaining the supply of eunuchs to the Muslim world.

The highest rate of success when creating a eunuch is when boys who have not yet begun puberty are used. The shock to the system is less and the survival rate better. The prognosis depends also upon which methods are used and how extensive the operation is to be. In some of the earliest records of castration, the testicles are merely crushed and rendered useless. There is no loss of blood in such a process and although the pain would have been excruciating, the chances of it resulting in death would be minimal. The ancient Assyrians used this technique, as did the Italians when creating castrati, boy singers who were castrated to preserve their soprano voices (Feldman, 2015). Other relatively benign procedures include opening the scrotum with a small incision and then scoring the testicles until they are so damaged that they simply wither away. The mortality rate from operations of this kind is very low. Unfortunately, these methods did not fit the bill for the eunuchs required for service in Muslim palaces or harems. It was not enough for somebody to claim that a eunuch's testicles were useless and damaged beyond repair. Nor was it sufficient for the testicles to be removed. Before a eunuch could be used, an inspection had to be carried out to confirm that not only were the testicles and scrotum completely absent, but that the whole of the penis had also been amputated. More than that, periodic inspections were carried out to ensure that the penis had not started to grow back (Ayalon, 1999).

The reason for being so ruthless about the extent of castration is that even with the testicles removed, it is sometimes possible for a man to have an erection of such firmness that he is able to have intercourse. Radical castrations in which scarcely even the stump of the removed penis are left proved to be the most effective way of ensuring that the women of the harem were left unmolested by those whose duty it was to guard them.

Cutting off both penis and testicles can easily cause a person to bleed to death. Even if this does not happen, the risk of subsequent infection is very great. This was particularly the case before there was any clear understanding of how infection spreads and at a time when there were no antibiotics to treat it, even if it developed and was correctly diagnosed. This is one factor which greatly contributed to the high number of deaths from this treatment. One method devised to make amputations as clean and hygienic as possible, introduced another risk. This was cauterisation with a red-hot iron as soon as the body part had been removed, which prevented excessive bleeding by sealing up the open ends of the severed blood vessels. This worked well enough when cutting off a hand or foot, but was not practicable with radical castrations as it would lead to scarring and obstruction of the urethra. The possibility of scar tissue or strictures forming in the urethra and so preventing the bladder from draining was in any case high. If this happened, then the bladder could simply burst, with consequences which were invariably fatal. If, three days after the operation, the man or boy was unable to urinate then, 'the passages have become swollen and nothing can save him' (Penzer, 2005). Metal plugs could be inserted immediately after the penis had been cut off, in an attempt to prevent the urethra from closing during healing, but this was still a chancy business.

Of course, if one bought a slave and he subsequently died of the effects of castration, then the price paid was simply lost. For this reason, rather than any humanitarian considerations, it was important to do the utmost to ensure that the victims of this barbarity survived their mutilations. It was to cater for this need that enterprising souls set up special centres in Europe where boys could be brought to be castrated. For two or three centuries, this was a flourishing industry in Italy and France.

Problems with the urinary tract, at least in the short term, could often be prevented by inserting a small plug in the urethra, immediately after the penis had been removed. This was kept in for three days and the boy not allowed to drink liquid or urinate during that time. When the plug was removed and urine flowed, then the danger of death by a ruptured bladder had passed. From then on, and for the rest of his life, the castrated boy would either have to sit or squat in order to urinate. Incontinence was a frequent disability and for some the plug became a permanent feature of their lives, only being removed when it was necessary to void the bladder. Many suffered leakage at other times and it was not uncommon for a eunuch to smell of urine.

There were various routes by which the slaves reached the European cities where the specialized castration centres existed. Since the great majority of the boys operated on were Slavs, they were usually brought down through what is now Russia and into Europe from the north. The Vikings captured prisoners in the Slav lands and then sometimes sold them on to other slavers who would bring them to Europe. Just as there was a prohibition in Islam on the castration of slaves, so too did Christianity frown upon the practice. Indeed, even trading in Christian slaves was unacceptable, which made the unconverted heathens from what is now Russia ideal for the purpose. Being neither Muslim nor Christian, nobody cared sufficiently about them to try and discourage the cruelties which were perpetrated upon them. Writing in the eighth century, Paul the Deacon described, 'innumerable troops of captives' being taken south from Slav lands and also what is now Germany (Foulke, 1974).

There is a curious circumstance associated with this trade and it is as follows. It is sometimes asserted today that the transatlantic slave trade was dominated in the eighteenth century by Jewish merchants. This is a debatable point, but no such uncertainty attaches to the role of Jews in the medieval slave trade, which largely involved the export of white slaves from Europe to North Africa. The reason for this is not difficult to ascertain.

For a thousand years or so, Christian Europe was at odds with the Muslim world of North Africa and the Middle East. Invasions took place in both directions. At one time, the Muslim armies swept across the Pyrenees into France and then, a few centuries later, European armies converged on the Middle East and occupied much of it, setting up Christian kingdoms in Jerusalem and other places. Four hundred years later, Muslim armies were marching through Europe and only halted at the gates of Vienna. All these military activities were, at least nominally, motivated by religious fervour; the desire to convert unbelievers to the one true faith of, depending upon one's origins and skin colour, either Islam or Christianity. It followed as a matter of course that Muslims travelling through Italy and France were viewed askance in just the way that Christians in Syria and Algiers would be. Jews, not being bound to one side or the other, could often travel and trade more freely. It was accordingly far easier for a Jew to transport slaves to Venice or Verdun and then on to Africa, than it would be for a Christian.

As early as the late fifth century AD, a pope gave permission for Jews to bring non-Christian slaves into Italy, from where they were then sent to North Africa. Pope Gelasius was appointed Pontiff in 492 and from the first year of his reign was happy to see Slavs and Germans brought south, *en route* to Africa. This was the beginning of extensive Jewish involvement in the slave trade. Within a century or two, the Jews were accepted as being the chief slave traders between Europe and Africa and the Middle East. A large part of their trade was in young men who had been brought to southern Europe to be castrated and then sold to Arab markets as eunuchs.

In the later ninth century the Arab writer Ibn Khordadbeh was giving a detailed account of the routes which were being used by those trafficking in slaves. In his work *Book of Roads and Kingdoms*, he gave a detailed and precise account of who was behind the trade and how they moved their goods to and from Europe. Most of the slaves were bought by Jewish traders in what is now Russia, Ukraine and the Balkans and then taken to Venice or Verdun to be operated upon. As Director of Posts and Police for a province of the Abbasid Caliphate, Ibn Khordadbeh was in the best possible position to know about such things (Meynard, 1865). The traders whom he wrote of were the Radhanites, a guild of Jewish merchants about the origin of which there are a number of theories. What is certain though is that the Radhanites were an international business, who travelled across Europe, Asia and Africa, dealing in luxury goods of high value. These men were multilingual and had bases across the whole of the known world, from Western Europe to the far East, from northern Russia to Africa. To quote Ibn Khordadbeh:

> These merchants speak Arabic, Persian, Roman, Frankish, Spanish, and Slav languages. They journey from West to East, from East to West, partly on land, partly by sea. They transport from the West eunuchs, female slaves, boys, brocade, castor, marten and other furs, and swords. (Meynard, 1865)

As we have seen, the Slavs were mostly heathens; that is to say they were neither Christians nor Muslims. As such, they were regarded as fair game by anybody who could catch them and take them from their homes. Russia and the Ukraine were good sources of Slav slaves and so were the Balkans, which were also populated largely by Slavs. Bosnia was especially convenient, for it had a coastline on the Adriatic Sea, a short journey by ship from Venice. The slave trade from Bosnia flourished for centuries, coming to an abrupt halt in 1463, when the Ottoman Empire invaded and occupied the area (Clarke, 1998). The loss of this important source of slaves was compensated for by the opening up of a new and larger, indeed seemingly inexhaustible, supply elsewhere. At about the same time that the Ottomans were taking over the Balkans and closing it off to European slave traders, the Portuguese were starting to exploit West Africa in a serious way. It was during the sixteenth century that the slave trade between Europe and Africa really took off. By 1540 some 12,000 slaves a year were being imported into Europe by the Portuguese. In Lisbon, the capital city, 10 per cent of the population were enslaved Africans (Grant, 2009). Who needed Bosnia, or indeed any Slavs, when Africa was apparently able to supply any demand?

Just to remind ourselves of the situation at which we have been looking, for black slaves in America and the islands of the Caribbean, castration was a rare and terrible punishment inflicted in exceptional circumstances. The castration of white children in Europe who were to be sold into slavery in North Africa or the Middle East was, on the other hand, a regular occurrence which took place over a period of centuries.

The continued demand in the Muslim world for large numbers of European slaves was to cause enormous problems on more than one occasion for the countries to which they were exported. Not one but two dynasties of slaves emerged in the Middle East which both toppled their supposed owners from their position of power and actually ended up dominating Egypt and the area which we know today as Iraq. The story of these powerful groups of slaves is a fascinating one and shows the dangers of relying too heavily upon men who are at the very bottom of the social order and have little or nothing to lose. We shall examine these strange societies, which grew to be very powerful in the Muslim world, in the next chapter. First though, let us consider a point which has already been briefly touched upon; the enormous influence which the trade in European slaves in North Africa had upon the subsequent history of the world.

So far, we have covered an aspect of history which is very probably quite unknown to the average reader. Very few people today are aware that Bristol was a centre for the slave trade before the Norman Conquest, nor are they likely to have heard of the white eunuchs and concubines who were taken from Europe to North Africa. The later African raids on Europe in search of slaves have similarly been forgotten. The effects of this trade though still reverberate through the world to this day. One or two concrete examples will make this plain. Britain's constitutional monarchy was established in the aftermath of the English Civil War. That is to say the delicate balance between the power of the Crown and that of the elected Parliament which exists today is largely a consequence of that conflict. The Civil War itself was triggered by a number of significant disputes, not least that over the payment of what was then known as Ship Money. This was bound up with the failure of the Royal Navy to protect England from the Barbary corsairs. The refusal of some important men to pay this tax was not only a cause of the Civil War, but was also the deciding factor in the choosing of sides when war did eventually erupt;

> The adherence of the sea-going population and of the Royal Navy itself to the parliamentary side of the quarrel bore witness to the patriotic character of Hampden's refusal to pay an illegal tax. (Trevelyan, 1942)

In short, the slave traders from Africa played a major role in the way that Britain's constitution developed.

The accession to power in 1958 of General de Gaulle, and all the political implications for the development of the European Union, also was a direct result of the struggle against the Barbary corsairs. The French invasion and occupation of Algiers in 1830 was the culmination of a low-level war fought with Algiers over the course of a century and a half. Again, the primary cause was the slavers operating out of Africa. Two more instances might also be of interest, touching as they both do upon the modern world.

We are familiar today with the spectacle of warships belonging to the United States sailing the world's oceans, maintaining and enforcing a particular vision of freedom and democracy. Similarly, the image of American troops operating in the Middle East is one which we have seen a good deal of on television and in newspapers over the last 30 years or so. It is strange to think that the very existence of the United States Navy as an international force owes its existence to the activities of the Barbary corsairs. Over 200 years ago, American marines landed in Libya, because the then president felt that Europe was not capable of sorting out a problem in the Mediterranean. Once again, this all-too-familiar scenario was bound up with the slavers of North Africa.

In 2015 columns of refugees, most of them Muslims, trekked north from the Middle East, heading into Europe. The response in western European countries like Germany was broadly sympathetic. Angela Merkel issued an open invitation for those thousands of men, together with small numbers of women, to come to her country, where they would be made welcome. The reaction of some countries laying on the route between the refugees and Germany was distinctly less positive. Some erected barriers and refused to allow any of the migrants into their own country. Hungary was one which took a hard line of this kind. Unless we are aware that Hungary was once invaded and occupied by Muslims streaming from Turkey and that young men from the Balkans and other areas were routinely carried off into slavery by Muslim rulers, we will not be able to understand what motivates the people now living in those parts of Europe. The terrible massacres which took place during the 1990s in the territories which made up the former Yugoslavia were also part of same historical pattern.

The Christian slaves from Europe at whom we shall look in the next chapter were not captured by the Barbary corsairs, but their enslavement was part of the same general pattern. They came from that part of Europe through which the refugees marched in 2015, that is to say the Balkans; Macedonia, Serbia, Croatia, Slovenia and so on.

Chapter 4

Mamluks and Janissaries

As the Arab nations of the Middle East grew strong and the centre of gravity of the Muslim world shifted from Mecca to Damascus, Cairo or Baghdad, those hoping to rule the vast territories which now stretched from India to the Atlantic coast of North Africa found that military power alone was the key to domination. The varying factions might put forward all manner of religious reasons why they should be the leading power and so command the loyalty of Muslims everywhere, but God, as has always been the case, was on the side of the big battalions. The problem with soldiers is that they can be fickle and disloyal and they often have aims and intentions of their own, which do not always accord with those of their supposed masters. They might, for instance, owe loyalty to their village or tribe, as well as having families for whom they wish to make provision. Perhaps they are greedy for riches or power. These personal interests can, given the right set of circumstances, override their allegiance to the leader whom they supposedly serve. The ideal soldier has no family, no nationality and no interest other than in fighting for his master. It was in search of such perfect fighting men that the rulers of the Muslim world struck upon the notion of creating an army of slave-soldiers whose devotion would be unquestioning and absolute.

History tells us that the creation of elite units in this way, whose only loyalty is to one particular individual, is fraught with hazard. One only has to remember Rome's Praetorian Guard, which was formed for a similar purpose. It did not take long before this unit was making and deposing emperors and became the real power in the land. Presumably, the Arab leaders who set out to create their own special groups of soldiers, separate from the rest of the military structure of the country, were not students of history.

The prohibition, found in the Hadith, on enslaving freeborn Muslims meant that for reasons of both religion and expediency, the acquisition of slaves for such an enterprise would have to be undertaken away from Muslim nations. From the ninth century onwards, young boys from countries which bordered North Africa, the Middle East and Persia were either purchased from slave traders or captured on raiding expeditions and brought to Arab countries to be trained as fierce warriors. They came from Greece and Albania, Armenia, the Russian Steppes, Sudan and the Turkish-occupied areas of Kazakstan. These youngsters were then taken to Muslim cities like Baghdad to begin their indoctrination. As soon as they arrived in their new home, they would be expected to learn Arabic and speak only that language, thus cutting one tie with their former lives. Most would never see their families again, nor their native lands. They were to be wholly dedicated to the leader who had bought them.

These slave-soldiers were known as Mamluks, an Arabic word meaning 'property' and one used as a recognized euphemism for slaves. For almost a thousand years, they were to play a crucial role in a number of Muslim countries, most notably Egypt. Their influence and power in that country was only broken for good when Napoleon Bonaparte arrived there with an army in 1798. The Mamluks first appeared though in Baghdad during the Abbasid Caliphate. Words such as 'caliphate' and 'Islamist' have over the last decade or so acquired exceedingly negative connotations in the West, due to their association with such things as the atrocities committed by the so-called 'caliphate' established by ISIS across much of Syria and Iraq. It might be helpful at this point to explain what a caliphate actually was and also why, contrary to popular opinion, 'Islamist' is not just another word for 'fundamentalist' or 'terrorist'.

Until his death in AD 632, the Prophet Mohammed was the acknowledged leader of all Muslims in the world. When he died, somebody was needed to replace him as the religious and political leader of the Muslim world. There was no distinction between temporal and spiritual authority at that time; the Prophet's successor would both rule Muslims in this world and also guide them as to the requirements and wishes of the Deity. This then is Islamism; a union of religious and political power so firm and indissoluble that the one cannot be separated from the other. Some Muslims today dream of restoring just such a system, first in the Middle East or Africa and then ultimately across the entire planet. Although this sounds a strange notion in the modern Western world, we must remember that it is exactly the state of affairs which existed in Europe until a few centuries ago, it being widely assumed that kings were appointed by God and that rebellion against the monarch was tantamount to launching an assault upon the Lord God himself. This was certainly the view of England's Charles I and he felt strongly that he was operating on God's behalf and that those opposing him were trying to overthrow the divinely-ordained system. A relic of this belief-system lingers on in the United Kingdom to this very day, because of course the head of state is also the head of the established church. Queen Elizabeth is, at least in theory, both our temporal and spiritual leader.

The successors of Mohammed were known as caliphs and the states and empires which they headed were called caliphates. There were four main caliphates and a number of others which existed contemporaneously, with varying degrees of legitimacy. These caliphates were based in different cities, such as Baghdad, Damascus, Cairo and Constantinople. One of the early caliphs belonging to the Abbasid Caliphate was Harun al-Rashid, a central character in some stories from the earliest version of the *One Thousand and One Nights* (Burton, 1885). His reign in Baghdad was part of the Golden Age of Islam and some of his activities have passed into legend. While he was alive, Harun al-Rashid hoped that the empire would be divided between three of his sons when he died, but in fact a bitter civil war broke out after his death in 809 between two of his sons who each wanted to have the entire empire under their control. Harun al-Rashid had many sons by different concubines and wives and one was the relatively insignificant Abu Ishaq, whose mother was a slave-concubine, meaning that he was himself scarcely legitimate. Nobody could have foreseen Abu Ishaq becoming the most powerful man in the empire, but he had a very shrewd idea.

Mao Zedong, the Chinese leader, famously observed that, 'Political power grows from the barrel of a gun'. In other words, to have political power, one must be backed by armed force. While his brothers were squabbling and then fighting about their inheritance, Abu Ishaq was building up his own personal army, which he was able to do at first without anybody noticing what he was doing. This is because instead of recruiting his soldiers from the streets of Baghdad, he was buying them, first in local slave markets and then overseas. His preference was, at least to begin with, for Turkish men. This requires a little explanation

Mention of Turkish people today means only one thing to most of us and that is that it refers to those who have their origins in the Republic of Turkey. Turkey, whose largest city, Istanbul, straddles the border between Europe and Asia, is widely, though incorrectly, assumed to be the native land of the Turks. In fact, the origin of the Turkish people lies thousands of miles from Turkey, in Central Asia. They come from the area of Mongolia and southern Siberia, rather than the edge of Europe. Two thousand years ago, the Turks were part of a confederation of tribes which had been raiding China intermittently for years. Like the Huns, who entered Europe to prey on the remains of the Roman Empire, the Turks set off on their own journeys, with some of them founding realms in Mongolia and what is today's Kazakstan (Haywood, 2008). The Turks were not at this time Muslims. Because they were not Muslim and lay on the fringes of the Caliphate, they were eligible, at least from the Muslim perspective, to be rounded up and sold as slaves.

Once he had a private army of perhaps 4,000 Turkish slaves whom he had trained to be a fearsome fighting force, Abu Ishaq threw in his lot with the elder of his half-brothers and helped him to win the civil war. As a reward, the new caliph made Abu Ishaq governor of Egypt and Syria. His Turkish troops were used to crush revolts and bolster his authority. When his brother died in 833, Abu Ishaq became caliph himself, ignoring the fact that his brother had left an adult son who could, and should, have inherited the title. A few years later, he had his nephew murdered by his Turkish soldiers and his position, militarily at least, was secure.

This then was the origin of the Mamluks who were to play such a crucial role in Muslim affairs over the coming centuries. Although the first Mamluks were Turkish, other nationalities were also recruited as time passed. Many of them were European. We are today used to the fact that there is a sharp separation between Christian Europe and the Muslim world of Asia and North Africa. Essentially, the Muslim world begins at the Bosporus, the straits which separate the two parts of the city of Istanbul. In the past though, large swathes of Europe were either ruled by Muslims or were under the influence of Muslim leader. This accounts for the Muslims in Albania, Bosnia, Bulgaria and Russia. It was from these areas that the Mamluks were increasingly drawn. A very large proportion were Slavs.

We pause at this point to consider an interesting linguistic point, which is that our word 'slave' is derived from the ethnonym 'Slav'. The first use of the word 'slave' in English is to be found in the late thirteenth century. It had at that time an extra letter and so was spelled 'sclave'. This spelling gives us a hint as to the word's origin. It is an anglicised form of the Latin word 'sclavus', which meant 'Slav'. The Latin word was an adaptation of the Slavs' own name for themselves, which was 'Sklavos'. This is, incidentally, cognate with the modern English Slovenian. From the Middle Ages onwards, Slavs and slaves were regarded as being pretty well interchangeable and the Slavs, the ethnic group who inhabited the Balkans and southern Russia, were seen as a natural group to pick on for anybody from the Vikings to the Arabs who wanted new slaves.

Although using foreigners who had no connections in the country in which they now lived must have seemed a brilliant idea at the time, in retrospect the risks of building up such a powerful military force appear obvious. True, they would have no loyalty to any faction in the Muslim lands and would be unlikely to start intriguing with this group or that in Baghdad or Cairo, but on the other hand, they often felt a strong loyalty and esprit de corps to their own unit and to each other. They had been taken from their own homes and countries, brought thousands of miles to a completely alien civilization and were now all thrust together into each other's company. It should not have been hard to foresee that a bunch of men all speaking Turkish or Greek would be likely to forge bonds with each other which were stronger than anything they might feel towards their Arabic-speaking Muslim owner.

Although nominally slaves, the Turkish guards who Abu Ishaq recruited were heavily armed and aware of their own importance. Shortly after coming to power, Abu Ishaq moved his capital from Baghdad to Samarra. The chief reason for this was that his Mamluks were regularly causing friction with the Arab citizens of Baghdad. In wartime, such men were exceedingly useful, but during peace, they became more of a liability. So it was that a campaign was launched against the Byzantine Empire, which occupied what is now the modern country of Turkey. Perhaps the Turkish troops took a liking to the area, for it is where they ultimately settled.

It took only a few brief decades before the dangers of the Mamluk scheme were starkly revealed. In 861 AD, just under 20 years after the death of Abu Ishaq, the Mamluks in Samarra murdered the caliph al-Mutawakkil. Six months later, they poisoned his successor al-Muntasir, following which the next caliph to be appointed, al-Musta'in, fled to Baghdad to try and rally support. In the meantime, the Mamluks had chosen and installed a caliph of their own whom they felt would be more favourably disposed towards their interests (Gordon, 2001). With their new leader, al-Mu'tazz, Baghdad was besieged by the Mamluks and al-Musta'in deposed and murdered. The Mamluks' chosen figurehead soon proved to have ideas of his own and one of these was to bring the military under control and restore the authority of the caliph. In the summer of 869, the Mamluks murdered him as well. The next caliph, al-Muhtadi, also tried to assert his authority and the following year, he too was killed.

It is worth remembering at this point that the Mamluks were supposedly slaves and yet within a matter of a few decades they had ended up choosing who should or should not rule the Muslim Empire. One sultan observed despairingly that he felt himself to be a slave of his slaves. Once such a degree of power has been attained, it was inevitable that the Mamluks should ask themselves why they needed to rule via a proxy, that is to say by supporting some leader or other and installing him in position. Why not simply rule by themselves? The result was that the Mamluks, formerly slaves, simply took over the Caliphate and ruled for centuries; first in Baghdad and then, after that city fell to the Mongols in 1262, from Cairo. The life of one such former slave might be instructive.

Between 1223 and 1227 a boy was born in one of the Turkish tribes living in what is now the Ukraine. He grew to be a young man whom we now know as Baibars. After fighting with the Mongols who were menacing both Europe and the Middle East at that time, Baibars and his tribe moved west and settled in Bulgaria. When he was in his mid-twenties, the Bulgarians fell out with Baibars' tribe, attacked them and sold many of them into slavery. Baibars was transported in chains to the slave market in the Syrian city of Aleppo. He ended up in Cairo, as a soldier of the sultan. Proving himself to be a very able military commander, Baibars led the armies of the sultan to victory against both the Mongols and the Crusaders from Europe who were trying to establish their own dynasties in the Middle East. Following his military successes, the sultan whom he was serving died in mysterious circumstances and Baibars the Mamluk commander promptly had himself declared sultan. He was still only in his thirties.

George Santayana once remarked that those who do not remember their history are doomed to repeat it and nothing could be more apposite when we observe what happened in the Ottoman Empire. Although most of us have heard of the Ottoman Empire, the meaning of the word 'Ottoman' is likely to be obscure and so a brief explanation might be helpful. 'Ottoman' is an Anglicised corruption of Osman, who founded a nation in what is today Turkey. Osman was himself Turkish, although his family actually came from Central Asia, fleeing attacks from the Mongols. It has been suggested that Osman I, who founded the Ottoman Empire, would actually have been called Attman, more in keeping with his Turkish origins, and that he is known as Osman because that name sounds more Arabic. Whatever the truth of the matter, at the end of the thirteenth century Osman founded his own country in a corner of the Anatolian plateau of central Turkey. Over the centuries, this nation expanded into a mighty empire which reached from the Afghanistan in the east almost to the Atlantic in the west. The general term, both for the empire and those who ruled it, was Ottoman.

Many of the early Mamluks were of course Turkish and their recruitment ended in a Mamluk dynasty which lasted for centuries. One might have thought that if any group would be able to benefit from studying this historical episode, it would have been the Turks themselves. Having seen the corrosive effect which the rise of the slave-soldiers had on existing systems of government, one might assume that they would be careful not to fall prey to the same foolish desire for a special corps of soldiers, fanatically devoted only to one leader. It might further be guessed that the inherent dangers of raising slaves to a position of such military importance would be glaringly obvious to the Turks. One would be quite wrong.

Because slaves were such an important commodity in Muslim countries at that time, like gold, spices or ivory, they were taxed by the government. In the case of slaves, taxation was in kind; that is to say, anybody importing slaves was liable to hand a certain proportion of them over to the ruler. Sometimes this was the sultan of the Ottoman Empire, but in the provinces of North Africa, the local governor might take his own cut. This meant that between a fifth and an eighth of the slaves brought into the Muslim world from Europe and Africa ended up as the property of the state rather than any individual owner. Some were, or became, eunuchs, others were concubines and a number ended up as galley slaves. Fifty years after Osman I founded his new country, it struck one of his successors as a good idea to start building up a personal bodyguard, a little like the Praetorian Guard of the Romans and very similar to the Mamluks, whose creation had caused so much trouble in the Arab world. His aim was recruit men loyal only to him, who would protect him from the troops of any discontented nobles or tribal chiefs. This unit was called the *Yeni Ceri*, or new corps, of which 'Janissary' is an English corruption.

To begin with the new body, the Janissaries, were formed from prisoners of war captured in the ordinary way. The prohibition on the enslaving of other Muslims was strictly adhered to at this time and so after a few years it was decided to collect non-Muslim slaves especially for the purpose of enrolling them as Janissaries. The younger that these boys were when taken, the better they would be likely to adapt to their new life. Grown men had the disadvantage of having wives and children to whom they might wish to return. A child of eight or nine would hardly be in a position to try and escape though and even if he did, would be unlikely ever to find his way hundreds of miles back to his own country.

So it was that in the 1380s the system of devshirme was instigated. During the devshirme, a word meaning gathering or harvest, representatives of the sultan scoured Greece and the Balkans every five years, aiming to take healthy and intelligent boys between the ages of eight and 14. Boys being taken from their families in this way and carried off into slavery may be seen in Illustration 9. They were taken to Constantinople, where they were circumcised and then converted to the Muslim faith. It will be observed that once again, it was the Slavs who were victim of slave raids, for that is what the devshirme effectively was. The children were seized from the countries which make up modern-day Serbia, Bosnia, Croatia, Slovenia, Albania, Macedonia, Bulgaria and Greece. The repercussions of those events echo down to the present day. During the fierce fighting in the 1990s between the countries which had once made up Yugoslavia, some of the worst atrocities were committed by Slavs against Muslims. In July 1995, 8,000 Muslims were slaughtered by a Serb militia who were determined to use ethnic cleansing to ensure that an area of Bosnia contained only Christian Slavs. The bitterness between Muslim and Slav has been a feature of that part of Europe for well over a thousand years and has its roots in the devshirme.

Since we will have occasion to mention the capital city of the Ottoman Empire again, a word or two might not come amiss at this point to explain why it is referred to throughout this book as Constantinople, rather than the Turkish name Istanbul. For almost a thousand years a Greek city stood where the Turkish city of Istanbul is now. This city, Byzantium, was razed to the ground by an angry Roman emperor for supporting the wrong side in a struggle for the throne. In AD 324 the Emperor Constantine decided that the Roman Empire could do with a new capital, Rome being too far from the borders of the empire for his taste. In an act of almost unbelievable vanity he called the city which he had built on the ruins of Byzantium after himself, naming it Constantinople. Even when this city eventually fell to the Turks, they continued to call it by their own version of Constantinople, which was Kostantiniyye. The common vernacular term for the city, Istanbul, was a garbled version of the Greek 'eis tin polin', which means 'into the city'. This name was not formally adopted in Turkey until after the end of the First World War.

Once they were in Constantinople, the boys gathered in the devshirme were educated and fully assimilated into Turkish culture. Not all of them were destined to become Janissaries. Some would, but others were trained for government posts in the civil service or even as political leaders. This was a very strange state of affairs, that the Ottoman sultans felt safer with foreign slaves who were converts to Islam having great power than they did men or their own nationality who had been born into the faith. Such slaves regularly rose to very high posts in the empire, sometimes ending up with more power than the sultan himself.

Ruling a great empire is no easy task for one man to accomplish and so the Ottoman sultans appointed advisers to whom they could turn and who, on occasion, were entrusted with running the empire on behalf of the sultan. These men were called viziers and the most important was the Grand Vizier. His position was roughly equivalent to the United Kingdom's Prime Minister, in that he ruled a nation or collection of nations on behalf of his sovereign. It is a curious and indisputable fact that the sultans preferred to entrust this vital role to foreign slaves, rather than any of their own people.

To begin with the Ottomans chose, as seems only natural, Turks to be their chief advisers and to rule in their stead. From 1320 to 1453, eleven Grand Viziers served the sultans, all of them Turkish. Then, something strange happened. Of the next six Grand Viziers, five were Greek and two Albanian. All were slaves or former slaves. This abrupt change seems puzzling at first sight but ties in with the reasons for recruiting both Janissaries and senior civil servants from among the European slaves. The man who held the post of Grand Vizier from 1439 to 1453 belonged to a very powerful and influential Turkish family, the Candarlis. He was the fourth member of his family to hold the post, his father, uncle and grandfather all having been Grand Viziers in their turn. The Candarli family had become so strong that it was beginning to look to the sultan, Mehmed II, that they were becoming a hereditary dynasty to rival the sultanate. He accordingly ordered the execution of his Grand Vizier and replacement with a Greek slave, one who had been gathered during a devshirme. Here was a man with no connections in Constantinople, no rich family backing him up or intriguing on his behalf. He held the post solely due to his ability. This began a long tradition in Turkey.

For the next 250 years, there was hardly a single Turk to be found among the Ottoman Grand Viziers. Plenty of Albanians and Greeks, Armenians, Bosnians and Hungarians, but there was a distinct reluctance on the part of successive sultans to allow any Turk so near to the levers of power. It was a similar situation in many more minor governmental posts, with foreigners tending to be more trusted than Turks. As with the civil administration, so too with the military.

Before looking at the Janissaries, we might stop and consider the nature of slavery itself a little. The life of the civil servants in Constantinople, or the elite troops who made up the Janissaries, was very different, and infinitely more pleasant, than that of the eunuchs at whom we looked in the last chapter. It was far better too than the existence of the galley slaves, about whom we shall be learning in later chapters. Nevertheless, all had one thing in common; they were slaves, being held against their will and forced to live and work for a master whom they had not chosen. Slavery need not necessarily be brutal or oppressive, but however mild the conditions of bondage, it is still slavery.

The Nazis were very enthusiastic about the use of slave labourers and at the Nuremburg trials held after the end of the Second World War, some of those who had captured and employed slaves were called to account. Between April and November 1947 the so-called WVHA trial was held, in which SS Lieutenant General Oswald Pohl of the Economic and Administrative Office of the SS, together with seventeen of his subordinates, went on trial for using slave labour. The defence emphasized that in many cases the slaves were fed and clothed to the same standard as the soldiers guarding them and that there had been no cruel mistreatment. The idea that this in any way mitigated the crime of enslaving men and women and forcing them to work was dismissed by the presiding judge, Robert Toms of the Circuit Court of Michigan. In delivering his judgement, he said;

> Slavery may exist even without torture. Slaves may be well fed and well clothed and comfortably housed, but they are still slaves if without lawful process they are deprived of their freedom by forceful restraint. We might eliminate all proof of ill treatment, overlook the starvation and beatings and other barbarous acts, but the admitted fact of slavery – compulsory uncompensated labour – would still remain. There is no such thing as benevolent slavery. Involuntary servitude, even if tempered by humane treatment, is still slavery.

We might keep these words in mind when reading of any apparently 'benevolent' slavery, such as slaves who become administrators of an empire or important soldiers. They were, for all that, still slaves.

Some of the boys collected in the 'gathering' ended up in the palace and other institutions, but many more became Janissaries. It was the third of the Ottoman rulers, Murad I, who first formed a corps of Janissaries during his reign, which lasted from 1362 to 1389. At first, he recruited them from prisoners of war and ordinary slaves. He soon found though that such men already had other loyalties and devotions and so before long the plan was devised that children would be taken from their own countries and specifically raised to the service of the sultan. The Janissaries had no other loyalty but a personal one to the ruler of the empire. This at least was the theory. In practice, just as with the mamluks, things worked out very differently.

At first, the Janissaries were subject to strict discipline and were indeed a fearsome military force. They were forbidden to marry, which it was hoped would also stop their loyalties being divided or their attention being distracted from the important matter of warfare. As their reputation grew, however, so the Janissaries became emboldened to make demands regarding the conditions under which they served. With the various foreign adventures upon which the Ottomans regularly embarked, aimed at expanding their territory, the crack regiment which spearheaded advances was seen as vital to the empire and it was thought worthwhile to make concessions to these fierce warriors, lest they should mutiny. In time they were allowed to marry and then to have their children admitted to the corps. Their numbers increased too. In 1400, there were perhaps 1,000 Janissaries, but by 1592 there were 23,232 (Ágoston, 2014).

It is almost inevitable that when a ruler relies too heavily upon an elite body upon which his very position depends, then the stage is set for difficulties, either for him or his soldiers. So it was with the Ottoman sultans and their Janissaries. Foreign slaves they might be, but they gradually came to rival the Turkish aristocracy in power. By the early years of the seventeenth century, they had become a serious threat to the stability of the empire (Balfour & Kinross, 1977).

They were now able to rid themselves of any sultan to whom they took a dislike. Osman II, for instance, became sultan in 1618 at the age of 14. Although young, he realized that he was in effect at the mercy of the Janissaries and complained that he was subject to his own slaves.

He laid plans to curtail the power of the Janissaries, starting by closing down the coffee houses of Constantinople, the places where most conspiracies against the throne were hatched. It did him no good, for when the Janissaries were sure that he intended to disband them, they arrested the young sultan and had him murdered.

It was to be over 200 years before an Ottoman sultan was finally able to break the power of the Janissaries. By this time, the once-elite fighting corps had expanded to 135,000 men and their wages bill was an enormous drain upon the empire's finances. In 1826 Mahmud II launched a war against them, using his regular troops. The barracks of the Janissaries were shelled with artillery, killing thousands of them.

We have looked in this chapter at some very special European slaves, whose lives were not terribly arduous and who in fact ended up being more powerful than their owners. Most of the slaves taken by Muslim raiders and acquired through trade were not so fortunate. Perhaps the worst fate was that which ended with men being consigned to the galleys for years, sometimes for the rest of their lives. This was not uncommon for those who were taken by the corsairs whose ships were a scourge in the Mediterranean and North Atlantic and we will now consider the way in which galley slaves were acquired from European countries, including of course the British Isles. Before doing so however, we might reflect upon what we learned in this chapter.

The Ottoman Empire, the Muslim caliphate which only came to an end after the First World War, was ruled, on behalf its sultans, by a succession of Grand Viziers, many of them more effective leaders than the sultans whom they nominally served. The majority of these men were not Turks, but rather came from the Balkans and neighbouring areas. They were Albanians, Greeks, Georgians, Hungarians, Bosnians and Serbs. The last Grand Vizier but one of the Ottoman Empire, who held the post in 1920, was a Bosnian Muslim. Another thirty earlier Grand Viziers had been Serbs.

The slave raids known as devshirmes, the conversion of large parts of the Balkans from Orthodox Christianity to Islam and the fact that for many years it was men from the Balkans who actually ruled the area on behalf of a Muslim potentate left an unpleasant legacy in the twentieth century. It will be recalled that the First World War began in Bosnia and was triggered by a Serb assassin. Following the death of Marshal Tito in 1980, Yugoslavia, the country which he had ruled over since the end of the Second World War, began a slow-motion collapse into chaos, civil war and genocide. Those who had no knowledge of the such things as the gathering of Slavs from the Balkans as slaves and the role of Muslims in this activity, were hugely puzzled by the terrible events of the 1990s. Surely, these people were all neighbours, who had lived happily, side by side, for many years? Whatever could be causing the atrocities which came thick and fast once the series of wars picked up pace? One incident in particular was seen as being almost uniquely horrible; the massacres which took place over a period of ten days at the Bosnian town of Srebrenica.

As part of the wars which followed the disintegration of the Federal Republic of Yugoslavia, a bitter conflict broke out in Bosnia in 1992 between the Serbs and Bosniaks who lived there. This culminated in July 1995 with the massacre of over 8,000 Bosniaks, Bosnian Muslims who had been living in the region alongside their Serb neighbours for centuries. This act of genocide was carried out by members of a Serb militia, who were Christians. Such barbarism did not erupt in a vacuum. The war brought forth all manner of simmering resentments and tensions which had been fermenting in that part of the world since the Middle Ages and as soon as suitable opportunity presented itself, then it seemed only natural for members of the Orthodox Church to fall upon Muslims living in the same province and butcher them mercilessly. It was said in the introduction to this book that a good deal of the history of the world and many modern events have their roots in the Muslim slave trade and this is a perfect example of what was meant by the statement. Far from being a random and spontaneous act of violence, the massacre at Srebrenica was the logical conclusion of events which took place 700 years ago.

We have looked closely at two of the groups of slaves who had a powerful effect first upon the Arab world and then the Ottoman Empire. This has been interesting for its own sake, in that we saw how European boys and girls were snatched from their own countries to serve the purposes of a Muslim nation. It has also been necessary to sketch the rise of the Ottomans, because unless we understand something about them, we will not be able to make any sense of the events at which we shall be looking in the next chapter, the seizure by men sailing from Ottoman ports of over a million European slaves from countries as diverse as Italy and Spain, England and Iceland, France and Ireland. These slave-raiding expeditions only took place because of the peculiar set of circumstances which existed at that time, as the Ottoman Empire expanded and began to encroach upon Europe.

Twenty-five years ago an American academic and political scientist devised a new method of analysing world history since the end of the Second World War. Samuel Huntington wrote a book called *The Clash of Civilizations* which advanced the hypothesis that the primary conflicts since 1945 has been driven not by ideological rifts such as that between Marxism and capitalism, but rather by cultural and religious differences (Huntington, 1996). This same model fits very well the situation which existed between Christian Europe and the Muslim Middle East as they came increasingly into conflict from the time of the first crusade until the sixteenth and seventeenth centuries.

The Crusades, which over a period of 200 years led to the capture of Jerusalem and establishment there of a Christian kingdom in the heart of the Muslim world, were religious wars launched specifically against the enemies of Christianity. So too were the invasions and incursions by the Arabs and Turks which led to parts of southern and eastern Europe being under the rule of successive caliphates. The Europeans adopted for their symbol the cross and the Muslims the crescent. Both civilizations hoped to extend the area which lay under the rule of their own religious and temporal leaders. It is in this context that the seizure of white Christians from Europe and their captivity in a life of slavery must be seen; as part of a continuing series of raids made by Europeans upon the Middle East and North Africa, and by the Ottomans upon Europe. These raids were carried out by seafarers who became known as the Barbary pirates.

Chapter 5

The Coming of the Corsairs

The words which we use to describe things can strongly influence how we view and think about them. By using humorous expressions, we can ridicule or mock something which is, in reality, malignant and dangerous. During the Second World War, cartoons and comic songs appeared about Hitler and the Nazis, although anything less amusing than the Holocaust and the other horrors of that conflict can hardly be imagined. Mention of the Siegfried Line today is likely to call to mind only the light-hearted wartime song *We're Going to Hang Out the Washing on the Siegfried Line.* That fact that over 140,000 men died fighting along the Siegfried Line has largely been forgotten.

Sometimes, choosing one word or the other to describe an event or series of events can have the inadvertent effect causing us to forget how dreadful something was. Mention the word 'pirate', for instance and our thoughts turn perhaps to Long John Silver, Captain Hook from *Peter Pan*, Captain Pugwash or Gilbert and Sullivan's comic opera *The Pirates of Penzance.* More recently, we have seen Johnny Depp's character of Captain Jack Sparrow, as portrayed in the *Pirates of the Caribbean* films. Just as with most other fictional pirates, Jack Sparrow is not vicious or depraved, but rather a vaguely humorous creation, more likely to cause amusement than he is terror or disgust. Pirates are picturesque and quaint. Perhaps this is one of the reasons why the slavers who once infested the seas around Britain have become forgotten, because they were described as pirates, rather than given their correct name?

Pirates are of course maritime outlaws, who live by plundering anybody's ships and seizing either them or the goods which they carry. Piracy has been a problem for the whole of recorded history. In 75 BC, Julius Caesar was captured by pirates in the Aegean Sea, off the coast of Greece, and held for ransom. He later tracked them down and crucified the lot of them. Right through to the modern day, pirates are still active and a menace to merchant shipping in several parts of the world. Those known as Barbary pirates fell into quite a different category being, according to how strictly one defines such things, either privateers or corsairs. Both words are slightly archaic and obscure, so a slight etymological detour is probably necessary.

Privateers are private citizens who command ships which are commissioned by a state to carry out acts of war. Britain made a lot of use of privateers, particularly in the sixteenth century. Some famous sea-captains and explorers of the Elizabethan period, Francis Drake and John Hawkins among them, operated as privateers from time to time. It is a useful way of supplementing one's naval forces, to offer individuals who own ships a chance to make money by fighting for their country. The rewards could be very great, as some enemy ships were carrying large amounts of gold or other valuable cargoes. The country which authorized the privateer, by providing what is known as a letter of marque, specified which nation's ships could be attacked and for how long the commission would last. A percentage of the plunder would be claimed by the ruler who had issued the commission.

As may readily be imagined, one nation's privateers are often regarded by opposing nations as little better than pirates. Francis Drake was certainly viewed in this way by the Spanish. There was also the possibility that a privateer might actually turn to piracy, by attacking other ships more or less at random, according to how much treasure they might yield. French privateers were known as corsairs, although the word became a more general one, describing daring privateers from other countries apart from France. The Barbary pirates were sometimes known as Turkish corsairs, The coast of North Africa was nominally under the rule of the Ottomans and so those living there were often described, quite erroneously, as Turks.

The Barbary pirates or corsairs came from the North African coast which was, as we saw in an earlier chapter, at one time the home of the Berbers, after whom the Barbary Coast was named. The state of affairs in North Africa requires some explanation. The Ottoman Empire covered an enormous area in the sixteenth and seventeenth centuries, reaching its greatest extent in 1683, by which time Turkish forces were besieging Vienna. At that time, the empire stretched from Iran and included a large part of the Middle East. The modern countries of Turkey, Iraq, Syria, Lebanon, Jordan, Israel, Egypt and much of Saudi Arabia were all under the sway of the Ottomans, as was most of Eastern Europe. Greece, Albania, Romania, Bulgaria, Hungary, Croatia, Slovakia and Serbia, as well as parts of the Ukraine and Russia, were all either directly under the Ottoman thumb or were vassal states. In North Africa, Tripoli, which was roughly where present-day Libya now exists, Tunis and Algiers were all autonomous provinces. Expressions such as vassal states and autonomous provinces might not be readily understood by some readers.

Almost all the people in the world today live in sovereign countries which is to say discrete, geographical locations with clear borders, which are governed by their own political system. Historically, this model, although common enough in Europe, was unusual. The rule tended to be more for empires and cultures which covered large areas and had changing and ill-defined boundaries, which were constantly shrinking or growing. The Ottoman Empire was a typical example of this kind of thing. In 1355, the Ottomans held sway over a small corner of what is now Turkey. Over the next three centuries, they slowly but inexorably swallowed up neighbouring territories such as the Byzantine Empire, until their writ ran from Baghdad to Vienna. Not all this vast empire though was ruled directly from the Ottoman capital of Constantinople, formerly Byzantium.

Some of the countries in the Ottoman Empire, Hungary for example, were free to run their own affairs as long as they acknowledged Constantinople's authority over them. These nations were known as vassals. Then there were the areas of North Africa which had been conquered by the Arabs in the years following Mohammed's death in 632. These territories were named after their chief cities; Algiers, Tunis and Tripoli. They were autonomous provinces of the empire and although they technically owed allegiance to the Ottomans, they were in practice often like independent countries. Tripoli had been held by the Spanish for a few decades of the sixteenth century, but from 1551 onward, it was part of the Ottoman Empire. Because of their affiliation with the Ottoman Empire, those living in those regions were often erroneously known as Turks and those prisoners and slaves who, to advance their prospects, converted to Islam were said to have 'turned Turk'.

The Barbary provinces were ruled over by men who were nominally exercising authority on behalf of the sultan in Constantinople. Some were known by the title of 'Pasha', while in Algiers the head of state was known as the 'Dey'. Sometimes rather than 'Dey', the ruler was called the 'Bey'. Similarly, because Arabic has no letter 'P', the title 'Pasha' is from time to time rendered as 'Bashaw'. All we need to remember is that all these words mean roughly the governor or de facto ruler of a city or large area of land.

One way of distinguishing privateers and corsairs from pirates is to look at the way that they are viewed in their own country. Francis Drake was of course welcomed at English ports, although he might have received a somewhat frostier reception had he tried to sail into Cadiz. In the same way, the corsairs which sailed from the Barbary provinces were regarded in their own ports as being legitimate fighting vessels, on a par with the regular naval forces. In effect, the corsairs who raided Europe were really an extension of the naval power of the provinces and countries from which they sailed. Just as the English used privateers to attack the Spanish Empire, so did the Ottomans and their client-states use their own privateers to harass the Christian countries with whom they believed themselves to be at war.

The aim of the heavily-armed ships which sailed from the ports of Algiers, Tunis and Tripoli was to launch raids against both Christian countries and shipping in Europe. They were after plunder and in particular to collect slaves to be sold in Africa and the Middle East (Syed, 2011). Their ships sailed quite openly from bases in North Africa and the civil rulers of the territories from which they made their forays claimed a certain percentage of the slaves whom they captured. Because they were operating on behalf of certain countries, rather than as independent marauders, the Barbary corsairs did not need to operate on a small scale, as pirates generally did, but would combine in huge fleets to take part in coordinated actions. In 1544, as the Ottoman Empire was reaching the peak of its power, the island of Ischia in the Gulf of Naples was attacked and 4,000 of the inhabitants carried off to Africa as slaves. The same year, Lipari, an island off the coast of Sicily, was raided and between 2,000 and 7,000 people taken as slaves to Tripoli (Syed, 2011). These were not pirate raids, but military operations. The logistics of taking thousands of people prisoner and then transporting them to another continent required many ships, a large force of men, careful planning and the willing cooperation of those in charge of the countries to which the captives were taken. These operations were not acts of piracy, but rather combined military actions by an army and navy.

Although the expression was not coined until the Second World War, the removal of entire populations from islands in the Mediterranean may best be regarded as an instance of ethnic cleansing. Depopulating areas of Christians made perfect sense for a nation intent upon expanding both its territory and religion. The Ottomans were engaged in open warfare with Venice and both sides took any chance they could to disrupt the other's trade and influence. Physically removing Christians from islands on the Italian coast both demonstrated in a very direct and brutal way that the Mediterranean belonged to the Muslims rather than the Christians and also provided the manpower necessary to propel the galleys of the Muslim ships. This may be seen with great clarity when we look at the events leading up to the siege of Malta in 1565, of which the attack on the island of Gozo was a prelude.

The great mistake in calling the corsairs sailing from the Barbary Coast 'pirates' is that this suggests that they were individuals operating for their own profit and advantage. They were not. Like any rational people, they wished to make a living, but they did so as part of a recognized strategic campaign, the object of which was the subjugation of Europe to the forces of militant Islam. This was to be achieved in the first instance by nibbling away at the edges, rather than by launching mighty assaults upon entire countries at a time. Targeting islands was an excellent way of pursuing such a plan.

Before the Ottomans turned their eyes west and regarded Europe as the logical next step in the conversion of the known world to Islam, the Arabs had already adopted a similar strategy a thousand years earlier. Cyprus was an early victim of this territorial expansion and Mohammed's aunt herself took part in an expedition to invade the island in 648. She fell off her mule, broke her neck and was buried where the accident occurred, just outside the modern city of Larnaca. Her tomb, in the Hala Sultan mosque, is one of the most important Muslim holy sites. Malta too was attacked by Arabs, as was Sicily. Both islands were occupied for a century or two, before being driven out by the Normans at the end of the eleventh century.

The Arab occupation of Malta had one curious and long-lasting effect; it is the only European country to speak a language based upon Arabic. However, this linguistic curiosity probably had no bearing upon the Ottoman decision to attempt to capture the island in the sixteenth century. All the Arabs had been expelled from the place years earlier and Malta's real attraction as a possible place to conquer lay in its size and geographical location. It is a tiny island, considerably smaller than the Isle of Wight, on Britain's southern coast, and also further west than any of the other Mediterranean islands in which the Ottomans had an interest. Occupying Malta would show that the Mediterranean truly belonged to the Turks, rather than the Venetians, French or Spanish.

The assault on Malta illustrates beautifully the way in which the corsairs and their actions tied in neatly with the aims of the Ottoman Empire. Rather than being outlaws, they were really more like pioneers; testing the enemy defences and discovering weak spots ahead of a full-scale military invasion by the official armed forces of the empire. It is in this context which we must examine the seizure of the island of Gozo in 1551.

Malta is not one island, but rather an archipelago, consisting of two main islands and a string of smaller ones. The second largest of the islands is called Gozo and it has an area of about 26 square miles. In 1551, the main island of Malta was held and defended by a Catholic military order called the Knights Hospitaller or, more correctly, the Order of Knights of the Hospital of Saint John of Jerusalem. In the thirteenth century they had been based in Jerusalem and had moved first to the island of Rhodes and then to Malta in 1530. Military orders of this kind were really a leftover from the Crusades and rather than fighting to expand Christian influence in the Middle East had now adopted a role of defending Europe from the rapidly growing Ottoman Empire. The Knights Hospitaller had had a base in Tripoli since 1530 and some territories of the Mediterranean changed from Christian to Muslim and back again as the Ottomans conducted what looked like their own crusades in the name of Islam.

Many writers describe the seizure of Gozo and the wholesale deportation of the Christians living there as being carried out by Barbary 'pirates', but this is of course absurd. It is difficult to imagine even a sizable company of pirates being able to cope with the problem of moving 6,000 men, women and children across the sea. What really happened was that privateers were working hand-in-glove with the regular Ottoman forces to effect the transfer of an entire population into slavery.

The sacking of the island of Gozo was in the nature of a consolation prize for the Ottomans. In 1551, a fleet under the command of Sinan Pasha approached Malta and landed 10,000 troops on the main island. This army then marched on the coastal town of Birgu. In addition to Sinan Pasha's ships, there was another force of corsairs, under the command of one of the most famous of the Barbary corsairs, a man known as Turgut Reis or Dragut. His nom de guerre was 'The drawn sword of Islam'. Only a couple of decades earlier, Birgu had been a small and defenceless settlement of ramshackle houses, with the chief means of subsistence being fishing. When the Knights Hospitaller arrived in Malta, they chose Birgu as their base and fortified it, building a castle nearby. When the Ottoman soldiers reached Birgu, they realized that only a prolonged siege would be of any use if they wished to take the town and so they moved on to the then capital, Mdina. This too had been reinforced and so the attacking troops decided that the case was hopeless. They returned to their ships and without wasting any time in regret, sailed at once to Gozo and captured it after a short bombardment from the sea. One of the defenders, a man called Bernardo Dupuo, saw that it was only a matter of time before the island was overrun. Rather than allow them to be taken into slavery, he killed his wife and two daughters, before dying in battle himself against the invaders.

On 30 July 1551 every single person living on Gozo, with the exception of one monk and a few dozen people who were so old and incapable as to be useless as slaves, were loaded onto the ships and transferred to Tripoli, where they were sold as slaves. Turgut Reis supervised this operation and landing in Tripoli he also disposed of a base of the Knights Hospitaller who had installed themselves there. Fifteen years later, the Ottomans returned to Malta in force and besieged it, an event known as the Great Siege of Malta. It was all in vain though, for the island did not fall.

We saw in the last chapter how the Caliphate shifted its base from Baghdad to Damascus and then Cairo. In the sixteenth century, the Caliphate was based in Constantinople, where it would remain until the end of the First World War in 1918. The fact that the ships from Africa were sailing on their expeditions quite openly from ports ruled by the Ottoman Empire, where the Caliphate was now established, gave the slave raids a religious dimension, as they were aimed solely against non-Muslim targets. This accounts for the fact that the exploits of the Barbary Pirates are sometimes known as the Marine Jihad (Syed, 2011). Although the capture and sale of slaves was a profitable affair, the corsairs were, when all was said and done, Muslims. Their victims were Christians. As the Ottoman Empire expanded on land, so the corsairs did their best to establish mastery over the coastal waters of Europe. In Chapter 4 we saw that any part of Europe which was under the rule of the Ottomans was considered a good place to seize young men to become Janissaries. The gathering of slaves in this case took place on dry land. The corsairs of the Barbary Coast were engaged in a precisely similar campaign by sea. It was not a case of a few lone ships conducting hit-and-run attacks on lonely and isolated spots; entire fleets were involved. According to some estimates, more than a million Europeans were captured in this way by slavers from North Africa (Davis, 2002).

The Ottoman Empire was a force to be reckoned with in the sixteenth century and indeed, at one point it looked as though Europe might fall to the forces of militant Islam, just as it almost did before the Battle of Poitiers in 732 (Castleden, 2005). At the Battle of Mohacs in 1526, the Ottomans crushed and then occupied the Kingdom of Hungary. This brought them within striking distance of Vienna and meant that a large part of Eastern Europe was now occupied by a Muslim power (Hibbert, 1970). Just as they seemed invincible on land, so too at sea. Little wonder that after a series of raids on England in 1625 and 1626 Sir John Eliot, Vice Admiral of Devon, said in frustration that the seas around England 'seem'd theirs' (Matar, 1998).

To begin with, the activities of the corsairs were limited to the Mediterranean Ocean and the countries surrounding it. Some parts of the Spanish and Italian coast became more or less abandoned, because those living there feared being captured by a raiding party and carried off to slavery in Africa. The danger though was not limited to those on dry land, because ships belonging to any Christian nation were also considered fair game. In 1577 an English merchant ship called the *Swallow* was passing through the Mediterranean and happened to sail a little too close to Algiers. Barbary pirates boarded the *Swallow* and took the crew off to sell as slaves. One of them met an especially grisly fate. Samson Rowlie was castrated, following which, for reasons which are obscure, he converted to Islam, eventually rising to become the chief eunuch and Treasurer of Algiers (Brotton, 2017).

There were probably two chief reasons for the increasing activities of the corsairs. One the one hand, the commanders of such ships had a personal and mercenary interest in what they were doing, much like privateers such as Sir Francis Drake. In short, they were largely in it for the money. For the Ottomans, who encouraged and more or less licensed and taxed the trade in Christian slaves, there was another motive. Showing that their ships could go wherever they wished and land in any country was a good way to demonstrate the power of the Ottoman Empire. The message was clear; they were unstoppable on land or at sea. This notion of the ubiquity and invincibility of Ottoman forces would be of great psychological benefit, or so it was thought, when a move was made to capture another part of Europe.

Apart from the obvious value of the captives who were taken and sold as slaves, there was another financial arrangement which could bring in more money to the owners of European slaves in North Africa. This was that their families might try and ransom them, in effect buy them back from those who had already bought them. Sometimes, collections were held to raise money to ransom captives held in Algiers or other parts of the Barbary Coast. On 4 February 1585 two Englishmen called William Moore and Robert Rawlin were freed from the galley in Algiers where they had been slaves. Their ransom had been paid as a result of a collection in London. A religious order called the Trinitarians or, to give it its full name, the Order of the Most Holy Trinity and of the Captives, had been started during the Crusades with the object of freeing prisoners of the Muslims. During the period that the Barbary corsairs were seizing prisoners wholesale across Europe, the Trinitarians begged money from all who would give it, so that they might negotiate the release of slaves for cash. As the years passed, this ransoming of slaves proved more of a money-spinner for the Barbary corsairs than simply selling those they caught on the open market. A man will be prepared to pay a certain amount for a healthy slave, depending upon the state of the market at the time. There is, however, no limit at all to what a loving family will pay out in order to recover a husband, father or son.

The Trinitarians were not the only religious order in the business of ransoming captives and freeing Christians from slavery. In the thirteenth century, as the Crusades were drawing to a close, the order of the Royal, Celestial and Military Order of Our Lady of Mercy and the Redemption of the Captives was founded, with the express aim of freeing those held by the Muslims. For just as militant Islam was a factor in the corsair raids and seizure of shipping, so too did the Christians viewed the whole business as a religious struggle between the one true faith and a bunch of heathens. More commonly known as the Mercedarians, the order of Our Lady of Mercy raised money and sent emissaries to the Barbary Coast to negotiate the release of prisoners. They saw this not just as a humanitarian activity, but also as a religious duty. After all, it was claimed with some cause that those carried off by the corsairs were only targeted because of their faith in Jesus Christ.

It is time to look closely at just what a life of slavery entailed for those who were snatched from their ships or homes in the ways at which we have been reading about. We have seen how eunuchs were in demand, but what else were slaves needed for? Because the Pasha or ruler of the port where the slaves were brought ashore was entitled to an eighth of them, many ended up as galley slaves. Most people have heard of galley slaves; few have any clear idea what this entailed.

Galleys are large ships propelled by oars. They were widely used in ancient times by various civilizations around the Mediterranean, from the Phoenicians to the Romans and Greeks (Davison, 1992). Because the oars used by the rowers must reach the surface of the ocean easily, galleys sit very low in the water. They are consequently not suitable for the high seas, as strong waves are likely to swamp them. The Mediterranean Sea though is generally calm and ideally suited for the operations of such vessels. Pulling on oars which are 30 or 35ft long and have about the same mass as a modern telegraph pole is obviously beyond the capabilities of one man and so three to seven men are assigned to each oar. They must all pull in perfect unison and it is back-breaking work.

One problem with galleys is that they will only work effectively if every man is at his place and working to maximum capacity. If half the rowers are absent because they are eating, drinking or have left their benches to open their bowels or urinate, then the ship will not be able to operate effectively. For this reason, from the time of the Roman galleys onwards, it was found more convenient to use slaves, rather than free men. If they were chained to their places and encouraged to work at their hardest by an overseer with a whip, then the galley would be at its most efficient. Of course, there were disadvantages too to using slaves. If the men at the oars were soldiers, then they could join in any battle. They would not need to be so carefully watched for any attempt to escape either.

Although galleys were still being used by the all nations bordering the Mediterranean in the seventeenth century, they were by this time giving way to sailing ships. The sixteenth century was the zenith of the galley and most were at that time rowed by slaves, both Christian and Muslim. Venice was a major power in the Mediterranean and so was the still expanding Ottoman Empire. Galleys were used as both warships and for trade and the demand for slaves to crew them was constant and unremitting.

One source of galley slaves was the many prisoners of war taken by both sides in the struggle for supremacy of the Mediterranean during the sixteenth century. For the Muslim countries of North Africa and the eastern Mediterranean, there was the tax which was levied on the Barbary corsairs, by means of which an eighth of their captives were taken by the ruler of the district from which they operated. The number of slaves needed for the Ottoman galleys was enormous, as can be seen from the last major battle between rowed ships, which took place off the coast of Greece in 1571.

A coalition of Catholic nations, known as the Holy League, hoped to prevent further expansion of the Ottomans into Europe. Both the Holy League, which included Spain and Venice, and the Ottoman Empire had large fleets of galleys. On 7 October 1571, the two fleets, over 400 ships in total, clashed at the Gulf of Patras. The ensuing naval engagement became known as the Battle of Lepanto, because that was the name of the base from which the Ottoman forces had sailed.

The tactical details of the fighting need not concern us. What is of interest is the number of Christian galley-slaves freed after the defeat of the Muslims. A total of 12,000 European Christians had been rowing the galleys. This gives some idea of the numbers of slaves needed by the Ottomans at this time, and sheds light also on why there was no real will to suppress the slave trade. The conditions in which the Ottoman galley slaves lived are almost unimaginable today and squeamish readers are advised to skip the next few paragraphs.

A typical galley might have twenty-five oars on each side and perhaps three to five rowers for each oar. To ensure that the ship moved forward at the correct speed, every one of those rowers would need to be seated on his bench and rowing at all times that the vessel was travelling. For this reason, the slaves were shackled in place and were therefore physically unable to move from their designated position. Keeping them chained constantly in one place served two important purposes. First, as we have said, it meant that every oar would be working at full strength at all times, but there was another very good reason not to allow the slaves to wander about at will. This is that with around 50 oars to a boat and sometimes as many as five rowers to each oar, it was not uncommon to have 250 slaves who had absolutely nothing to lose on board a galley. The chances of a revolt by such a large body of desperate men were always present in the minds of those commanding the ship. Far safer simply to keep them shackled permanently in their places. This meant that when the need arose to urinate or defecate, these men had no option but to do so where they were sitting.

It was said in the sixteenth century that a galley crewed by slaves could be smelled from as far away as a mile (Bridge, 1988). A moment's thought will soon confirm that this was unlikely to be an exaggeration. Imagine, if you will, hundreds of men confined in a narrow space and compelled by nature to open their bladders and bowels where they were seated, day in and day out, for years at a time. There was no provision for washing and so these men would never have the chance to wash off the stale sweat from their bodies and if any activity is likely to generation copious amounts of sweat, it is propelling a large and heavily laden ship through the ocean by muscle-power alone. The rowers spent their lives ankle-deep in human waste.

The logistics of freeing the oarsmen so that they could sleep would have been enormously complex. Not only was there no space anywhere on the boat for them to stretch out, there was still the terrifying idea of having unshackled slaves about. Either they would have attacked their guards or perhaps even jumped overboard in an attempt to escape. The solution was that they were left shackled at their benches, 24 hours a day, and had to sleep as best they could, sitting upright.

The only prospect of escape for the Ottoman galley slaves was that which freed 12,000 of them after the Battle of Lepanto, that is to say if ships of a Christian nation defeated the Ottomans. From time to time, raids were made by European nations on the ports where the galleys stayed in between voyages, but such events were not common. Some countries such as Spain and France also used convicted criminals as galley-slaves, a fate which is graphically shown in Victor Hugo's *Les Misérables.* In such cases a set time would be served; perhaps five or ten years. For the slaves of the Ottomans though, there was no limit upon their servitude. Once consigned to the galleys, they would labour there until they died. A more dreadful fate it is difficult to imagine.

One of those who fought against the Ottomans at Lepanto was Miguel de Cervantes, who wrote *Don Quixote*, which is generally regarded as the world's first novel. Cervantes led an arduous and difficult life. He was born 20 miles north of Madrid in 1547. In 1570 Cervantes left Spain and enlisted in the Spanish Marines, who were at that time stationed at Naples. For five years he was an active soldier, fighting in various battles against the Turkish navy. On 26 September 1575, as he was sailing home to Spain, his ship was attacked by corsairs and he and the rest of the crew were taken to Algiers and sold as slaves (Thorlby, 1969). He was to spend the next five years as a slave, before being ransomed by the Trinitarians.

Despite the operations of the Spanish navy, the corsairs of the Barbary Coast had more or less free rein in the Mediterranean. Their ships were agile and fast and the heavy, slow warships of the Europeans were no match for them. In the seventeenth century, they began to probe further and further from their home ports, leaving the Straits of Gibraltar and entering the English Channel, the North Sea and even the Atlantic Ocean. The south-east coast of England was an obvious and tempting target for them.

The people living on the coast of the West Country have a long tradition of seafaring. Francis Drake was born in Devon. The seas around Devon and Cornwall were full of ships of all shapes and sizes in the early years of the seventeenth century. Fishing was of course a major livelihood at that time and there was no shortage of merchant ships either. Some of these were travelling to and from the New World and there were rich pickings to be had. Not only were there valuable cargoes, but also crews who could be sold in the slave markets of Algiers and Tripoli. If there were not enough ships around to make an expedition worthwhile, then the villages and towns scattered along the edge of the sea could be raided and, if nothing else, there were sure to be men, women and children there who could be taken aboard and shipped to Africa. It is time to look at the slave raiding expeditions which were mounted against the British Isles in the seventeenth century, years before Britain became involved in the transatlantic slave trade from Africa to America and the Caribbean.

Chapter 6

The Raids on the British Isles

J ames I, the Scottish king who also, on the death of Elizabeth I, acceded to the throne of England, was not very keen on the navy. In fact, he neglected it during the 22 years of his reign to such an extent that the fleet which once defeated the mighty Spanish Armada was no longer able even to protect English fishing boats from the depredations of foreign privateers. This was a shocking state of affairs which indirectly helped plant the seeds which would in the course of time ripen into a dreadful civil war. We remember that when the English Civil War began in 1642, it was London and the ports of England which were initially most keen to pledge their opposition to the Crown (Trevelyan, 1942). They had not forgotten those decades of neglect by the king and also the suffering at the hands of the Barbary corsairs, with no navy to protect them. For over 50 years, any fisherman setting out on his business was liable to be seized and carried off into slavery and there seemed nothing that their rulers were either willing or able to do about it.

It seems almost beyond belief that this terrible period of British history could have been forgotten, but there it is. Let us look at some specific incidents from the time. Between 1609 and 1616, a total of 466 English ships were boarded and the crews taken to North Africa as slaves (Brown, 1970). In April 1625, three ships from Cornwall and one sailing from Dartmouth in Devon were captured by corsairs and their crews taken. The following month, an entry in the *Calendar of State Papers* lamented that, 'The Turks are upon our coasts. They take ships only to take the men to make slaves of them.' Because the Barbary Coast was part of the Ottoman Empire, whose caliph was in Turkey, all Muslims were regularly referred to in England at this time as 'Turks'. The bold seizure of English vessels was bad enough, but there was worse.

The Royal Navy not only seemed to be unable to protect English ships at sea, even those close to the coast, they could not prevent slavers actually landing and taking people onto their ships to be transported to the slave markets of Algiers. In August 1625, a raiding party landed at Mount's Bay in Cornwall. The villagers saw the ships at anchor and fled for safe to the local church, but this was not enough to save them. The slavers dragged sixty people out of the church, loaded them into their rowing boats and took them on board the waiting ships. They all ended up in the slave markets of North Africa. On the 12th of that month, the Mayor of Plymouth wrote to the Privy Council in London. He pleaded for assistance from the navy, because in 10 days, 27 ships had been taken and all the men on board, over 200 of them, had been made slaves (Dalrymple, 2004).

All this makes strange reading today. We are familiar with the rout of the Spanish Armada by the English fleet in the late sixteenth century and yet now we see that that same navy was seemingly quite unable to protect the English coast from the depredations of a handful of pirates! The problem was, of course, that both the numbers of ships from the Barbary Coast and their type, made it almost impossible to deal with them in the way that one would a conventional, European fleet like the Armada. Even without James I's neglect of the Royal Navy, the lumbering warships which had served England so well in the past would not have been much use against the raiders sailing out of Africa. This was essentially what is now known as 'asymmetric warfare', with small groups of ships darting in and out of British waters. The Royal Navy had large, heavily armed ships which would have been ideal when it came to conventional naval warfare, but they were not fast enough or sufficiently manoeuvrable to cope with these swift attacks.

Although we now describe the ships from Africa as 'pirates', that is not how they were seen at the time. With the Ottoman Empire gearing up for another assault on Europe by land armies, the raids by ships from Algiers and Tripoli could be better seen as probing attacks, which tested the ability of the European powers to respond to landings and attacks on shipping in their own territory. It must be borne in mind that these attacks on Europe from the sea were a counterpoint to Ottoman expansion on land. During the seventeenth century the Ottoman Empire continued to grow at the expense of Europe, with new territory being swallowed up from Russia all the way to Austria and almost to Italy. With memories perhaps of the Muslim invasion of France in the eighth century, the sultans in Constantinople continued to press west into Central Europe on land and to harry the coasts of Spain, France and England from the sea.

The boldness and frequency of the expeditions against the British Isles and other parts of Europe were really extraordinary. Sometimes, more than one ship would be attacked simultaneously. In 1634, two ships carrying goods from Minehead in Somerset to Ireland were attacked and the crews captured. At other times, the African ships would work like a wolfpack to take a ship which they had targeted. On 20 September, 1635, what were described as 'six Sali men-of-war' seized a ship near the Scilly Isles, which lie off the westernmost tip of Cornwall (Eliot, 1881). The following March it was reported that thirty-six ships from England, Scotland and Ireland had been taken and in June that year three fishing boats containing over fifty men had been captured 'between Falmouth and the Lizard' (Eliot, 1881). In August 1638 it was reported that 'Turkish men-of-war of Algiers' were operating in the English Channel. We see in Illustration 10 some Barbary corsairs approaching a ship which they hope to capture.

The fact that the ships slipping in and out of British territorial waters were being described as 'men-of-war' is significant. This was the term applied only to warships and not generally to pirate vessels. The English at the time recognized that these raids were tantamount to an act of war and that the ships were really representatives of a hostile foreign power; namely the Ottoman Empire. Just as English 'privateers' were used as a way by Queen Elizabeth of harassing enemy countries, chiefly Spain, with the possibility of 'plausible deniability' if they went too far, so too with the ships from the North African ports under control of the Ottomans. Referring to the ships which were raiding shipping around the British Isles at that time, one historian calls such piracy a 'secondary form of war' (Braudel, 1949).

In his *History of England*, G.M. Trevelyan has this to say on the subject of the English privateers of the late sixteenth century;

> Above all, Elizabeth abetted the piratical attacks of Hawkins and Drake on the Spanish ships and colonies, by which the fighting power of England was trained during the years of public peace and private war. (Trevelyan, 1942)

To what extent it might be permissible to compare the situation with the English privateers with those from the Ottoman Empire will be explored in a later chapter, but for now it is enough to observe that once Britain agreed to pay the countries of North Africa what amounted to extortion money, the attacks on shipping at once ceased. This suggests that the rulers of those provinces were quite capable of controlling the privateers when they wished to do so.

Although the main period of its expansion and growth had been reached by the middle of the seventeenth century, the Ottoman Empire was by no means a spent force, as may be seen by the Siege of Vienna in 1683, when for a time it looked as though the forces of militant Islam were once again poised to sweep into western Europe, as had almost happened during the occupation of Spain, almost a thousand years earlier.

Of course, England was not the only country to be hit at this time by raids by the corsairs. Mediterranean countries such as Spain, France and Italy had been used to this sort of thing for years. As time went by, the slavers ventured farther afield. Ireland, whose major cities such as Dublin, Limerick and Waterford had all been founded as slave-trading centres, was also hit. One notorious incident was what became known as the 'Sacking of Baltimore'. This was the subject of a dramatic poem by the nineteenth-century writer Thomas Osborne Davis;

> All, all asleep within each roof along that rocky street,
> And these must be the lover's friends, with gently gliding feet-
> A stifled gasp, a dreamy noise! "The roof is in a flame!"

From out their beds and to their doors rush maid and sire and
dame,
And meet upon the threshold stone the gleaming sabre's fall,
And o'er each black and bearded face the white or crimson shawl,
The yell of 'Allah!" breaks above the prayer, and shriek, and roar:
O blessed God! the Algerine is lord of Baltimore!

In 1631, Baltimore was a small village on the southernmost tip of
Ireland. In the middle of June that year a fishing boat captained by
a man called John Hackett had been boarded in the Irish Sea and,
fearing that he would be taken to a life of a slavery in North Africa,
Hackett struck a deal with his captors. In return for his own freedom,
he would guide them to a sleepy little village which they could take
by surprise and then catch as many victims as they pleased. On the
night of 20 June, he went ashore with the landing party and led them
to Baltimore.

A total of eighty-nine women and children and twenty men were
taken prisoner that night and endured a journey of 38 days before they
arrived in Algiers, where they were sold to the highest bidder. Some
of the men ended up as galley slaves. The children were separated
from their mothers and most converted to Islam. The women either
were employed as seamstresses or became concubines (Ó Domhnaill,
2015). In England, there was pressure on King Charles I to enter into
negotiations to secure the freedom of the slaves, but he refused on the
grounds that it would only encourage more such outrages in the future.
Only three women ever made it back to their own country. After the
attack, the remaining villagers moved to nearby Skibbereen, which
was a larger settlement and further from the sea. Baltimore became a
desolate place.

We looked in Chapters 2 and 3 at Ireland's long association with
slavery, the fact that the capital city was founded by slavers and the
patron saint himself formerly having been a slave. There is another
curious connection between Irish traditions and slavery. The Claddagh
Ring is a quintessentially Irish piece of jewellery, which features two

hands holding a heart which bears a crown. The hands symbolise friendship, the heart love and the crown loyalty. Although the name 'Claddagh Ring' dates only from the 1830s, the design itself is known from the late seventeenth to early eighteenth centuries and an interesting legend is attached to it.

In about 1675 a silversmith called Richard Joyce was on board a ship which had left Ireland and was heading for the Caribbean. It was intercepted by corsairs and all those on board were taken to Algiers. Joyce, by good fortune, found himself bought by a goldsmith who recognized his worth. For fourteen years, he remained in this man's workshop, until King William III succeeded in arranging for the release of all the English and Irish slaves in Algiers. Joyce's owner was devastated at the thought of losing the best craftsman he knew and tried to persuade him to stay, by offering him both a half share in the business and also his daughter's hand in marriage. It was to no avail. In 1689 Richard Joyce returned to Ireland and settled in the town of Rahoon. He brought with him a design upon which he had been working for years and produced the very first Claddagh Ring.

The corsairs did not limit themselves to operating in out-of-the-way corners of the seas around the British Isles. At times, they sailed up the Thames Estuary, as far as Leigh-on-Sea (Fisher, 1957). For some years, Algerians even established a base just a few miles offshore from Devon. Mention a pirate island and most of us picture a tropical scene, with palm trees and a burning, tropical sun. Lundy Island is not at all like that. It lies in the Bristol Channel and is part of the English county of Devon. A map of Lundy may be seen in Illustration 11.

The Island of Lundy has been inhabited on and off since the Bronze Age. Its present name was given to it by the Vikings and means, in Norse, Puffin Island. Throughout the Middle Ages, Lundy changed hands with startling rapidity, being claimed at various times by the Crown, the Knights Templar, the Earl of Lancaster and the Cistercian order. In 1627 a fleet of ships from the republic of Salé, in what is now Morocco, took control of the island and remained there, on and off, for years (Milton, 2005). It was this collection of Algerians and other assorted Ottomans and Muslim converts who undertook the sacking of Baltimore, at which we looked earlier.

Lundy is not a particularly impressive place, being just three miles long and half a mile wide. It is rocky and barren, although a wonderful refuge for seabirds. Its great advantage for the mixed bag of North Africans and other nationalities who settled there in 1627 was that the island commands the Bristol Channel. Many of the ships sailing to America and the Caribbean at that time travelled from Bristol and passed within view of the Island of Lundy. It was simply a question of following them until they were out of sight of land and then attacking. That the problem was a severe one can be seen from the *Calendar of State Papers*, which provides the following appeals to London in August 1625;

> Mayor of Poole to the Privy Council. Unless measures are taken, the Newfoundland fleet of 250 sail, having on board four or five thousand men of the western parts, will be surprised by the Turkish pirates. (*Calendar of State Papers*, 1860)

> On 12 Aug., the Mayor of Plymouth writes that there are general fears for the ships from Virginia and Newfoundland. Twenty-seven ships and 200 persons had been taken by Turkish pirates in ten days. (*Calendar of State Papers*, 1860)

If the many privateers which were striking at the shipping leaving and entering British waters had been sailing in a massed formation, then the problem for the English would have been greatly simplified. It would have been a question of a set-piece naval battle and an exchange of cannon fire. Of course, the navy was not as effective as it had once been but might perhaps have had a good chance in a traditional battle at sea. Nothing of the kind took place though, at least not at that time. The ships of the slavers were agile and could be far away by the time that word had been sent to the nearest base and ships despatched. It was not to be until four years after the end of the English Civil War that firm action was essayed against the Ottoman Empire.

With no real opposition in the English Channel, Irish Sea or Atlantic Ocean, it was perhaps inevitable that the enterprising corsairs would venture a little further afield. Almost incredible to relate, in 1627 two separate groups sailed 3,000 miles to Iceland, where they thought that the pickings might be even easier than they currently were in Western Europe. Because the Icelanders have always been a very literate nation, we have a most detailed account of these raids and their aftermath. Indeed, the attacks that year are chronicled in minute detail, as are the subsequent experiences of those taken prisoner and sold in Algiers.

The first group of ships to appear off the coast of Iceland were commanded by Jan Janszoon, the same Dutch convert who had attacked the Irish village of Baltimore. He and his men arrived on 20 June 1627 and took just a few dozen captives back to Algiers. Two weeks later, on 5 July, some Algerian corsairs turned up to try their luck. They made a more thorough job of things, taking 350 prisoners. By all accounts, these men behaved with great brutality (Hreinsson & Nichols, 2016). Here is part of an account written by an official who was responsible for drawing up a report on the affair at the time;

> Then they began to set fire to the houses. There was a woman there who could not walk, whom they had captured easily. Her they threw on the fire, along with her two-year-old baby. When she and the poor child screamed and called to God for help, the wicked Turks bellowed with laughter. They stuck both child and mother with the sharp points of their spears, forcing them into the fire, and even stabbed fiercely at the poor, burning bodies. (Hreinsson & Nichols, 2016)

Among the women taken was the young wife of a Lutheran minister called Reverend Ólafur Egilsson. He himself was in his sixties and the raiders did not wish to be burdened with him, because he was old by the standards of the time and unlikely to fetch a good price at market. However, his wife and 11-year-old son begged that he should not be separated from them and so he was also loaded on board the waiting ships. It is to the Reverend Egilsson that we are indebted for a vivid narrative about what actually befell those who were taken for sale in Algiers.

One detail which was confirmed by the Icelandic minister was that the Ottoman governor of Algiers had an official interest in the slave trade and that it was not merely the individual activity of a few lawless pirates. Although he greatly overestimated the rank of the Ottoman governor of Algiers, calling him the 'king', Reverend Egilsson wrote that;

> This market was next to where their local king had his seat, so that he would have the shortest way there, because, as I was told by those who had been there a long time, their King took from the captured people every eighth man, every eighth woman, and every eighth child . . . (Hreinsson & Nichols, 2016)

In short, the collection of slaves from Europe was an accepted practice for those running the Barbary States and was simply taxed like any other mercantile activity.

Because he was so old and more or less useless as a slave, the Algerians released the minister and sent him to Denmark to see if he would be able to raise money to ransom some of the prisoners. Iceland was not at that time an independent country, but rather a Danish colony. After a long and circuitous journey, lasting six months and taking in Italy, France and the Netherlands, the Reverend Egilsson eventually arrived in Copenhagen, only to find that the scheme of ransoming his wife and son and the other 350 slaves was a non-starter. Denmark was so involved in the Thirty Years War that there was no money to be had for such a purpose. Sadly, the minister had to return to Iceland alone. His wife and a few dozen others who had been taken prisoner were freed 10 years later, but for the hundreds of others, their destiny was to remain in North Africa for the rest of their lives. We shall see later that Denmark had a good deal of trouble with the Algerian corsairs and this culminated towards the end of the eighteenth century in the now forgotten Danish-Algerian war.

It is time to examine the situation in both England and the rest of Europe and try to see why it was seemingly impossible to tackle the constant raids from the Barbary Coast. For much of the period at which we have been looking in this chapter, Europe was being racked by one of the most costly wars in terms of human life that has ever been seen. The Thirty Years War, fought across central Europe between 1618 and 1648, resulted in eight million deaths from military action, starvation, illness and civil disturbance. Nothing like it would be seen again until the Second World War. The partly religious and partly political causes of the war need not unduly concern us here. It is enough to know that at one time or another almost every nation in Europe had a hand in the business. The Ottomans were delighted to see Europe tearing itself apart in this way and they were involved to a limited extent because of their hold over part of Hungary. Set against the mighty struggle between the Holy Roman Empire, the Spanish Empire, Scandinavia, the Netherlands and many German principalities and states, leading to millions of deaths, the loss of a few thousand sailors and villagers to Ottoman slavers was a fairly minor consideration. In other words, nobody could really be bothered to get to grips with the problem; they had bigger fish to fry.

One event in British history which was connected to the activities of the Barbary pirates in the first half of the seventeenth century was of course the English Civil War, which began in 1642. The association of the corsairs with the Civil War seems to have been faded from memory but is well worth looking at. It might with some justification be said that the actions of the Barbary corsairs played a key role in precipitating the confrontation between Parliament and the king which was to lead ultimately to civil war.

James I of England, as we have seen, allowed the navy to become neglected and run down (Trevelyan, 1942). When the Thirty Years War began in 1618, the Royal Navy was a shadow of what it had been under

Elizabeth, in the days when it had defeated the Spanish Armada. By the time that James died and his son became King Charles I, the navy was hardly 'fit for purpose', as we would say today. Since the twelfth century, coastal towns in England had had a duty to provide fighting ships for the defence of the realm. Over time, this obligation had been replaced with a tax known as 'Ship Money'. This meant that instead of actually building and fitting out warships, those in maritime towns paid the Crown to do so on their behalf.

Realizing that he had inherited a navy in urgent need of overhaul and requiring many new ships to bring it up to scratch, Charles I decided to levy Ship Money not just upon towns on the coast, but rather on every county in England. Because Parliament had not authorized this, the demand made in 1628 was viewed unfavourably and abandoned after stiff opposition. It was not the end of the matter and in 1634, when he issued another writ to raise Ship Money, Charles decided to claim that he wished to strengthen the navy to protect the country from the attacks of the corsairs. In fact, the king had signed a secret treaty with Spain to join them in their war against The Netherlands, which struggle formed part of the Thirty Years War. Knowing that this would not prove popular with those who were being taxed, he concealed his true purpose in wanting to revitalise the Royal Navy (Chisholm, 1911).

Charles' demand for money in October 1634 was limited to ports and required them either to provide a certain number of fully-equipped warships or to supply the treasury with their equivalent cost in hard cash. To raise this money, the citizens of the towns would be taxed according to their means. This time, the Ship Money was a brilliant success and brought £104,000 into the exchequer. The following year, the tax was extended to the entire country and was for the sum of £208,000, which was also grudgingly paid. When, in 1636, the same thing happened once more, it was clear that the king was going to use Ship Money as a form of regular and general taxation.

Several high-profile court cases were heard which centred around the refusal of some individuals to pay Ship Money. In 1640, a group of citizens in London sent a petition to the king, stating their grievances. Heading the list was Ship Money and the petition mentioned:

> The pressing and unusual Impositions upon Merchandise, Importing and Exporting, and the urging and Levying of Ship-money, notwithstanding both which, Merchants Ships and Goods have been taken and destroyed both by Turkish and other Pirates. (Besant, 1903)

Put plainly, they were saying, what is the use of our paying all this money for ships if the navy can't even protect shipping from the corsairs? Two years later, the English Civil War began and the question of Ship Money, and by extension the raids by the corsairs from the Barbary Coast, was a major factor in precipitating the conflict between Parliament and the Crown. It was upon the ports that the burden of raising Ship Money first fell and they felt aggrieved that despite paying such vast sums to the exchequer, their citizens were still being captured and taken off into slavery. Little wonder that these cities chose not to back the king when the Civil War began.

In this chapter we have looked closely at the problem posed by the ships from the Ottoman Empire and seen why they were able to get away with their activities for so many years. The Ottoman Empire was strong and profited from the raids by levying a proportion of the slaves captured and using them in the galleys and so on. Europe was divided and so were several individual nations, including England. It is time now to examine how the situation developed in the second half of the seventeenth century and the arrangements which were made with the provinces of the Barbary Coast to prevent their attacking ships from Britain and certain other nations.

The slave trade as most people understand it; black Africans transported across the Atlantic Ocean.

Christian slaves from Europe, on sale in a slave market in Algiers.

Mannier Hoe de Gevange Kristen Slaven tot Algiers verkoft worden.

European slaves in North Africa at the end of the eighteenth century.

Above left: English slaves on sale in Rome in the sixth century.

Above right: Black Africans being sold as slaves in nineteenth-century America.

Above left: The Hebrews as slaves in ancient Egypt.

Above right: Black African slave drivers alongside African slaves.

Above left: A fierce Viking warrior.

Above right: Young boys from the Balkans being taken to Turkey as slaves.

Barbary corsairs approach a ship.

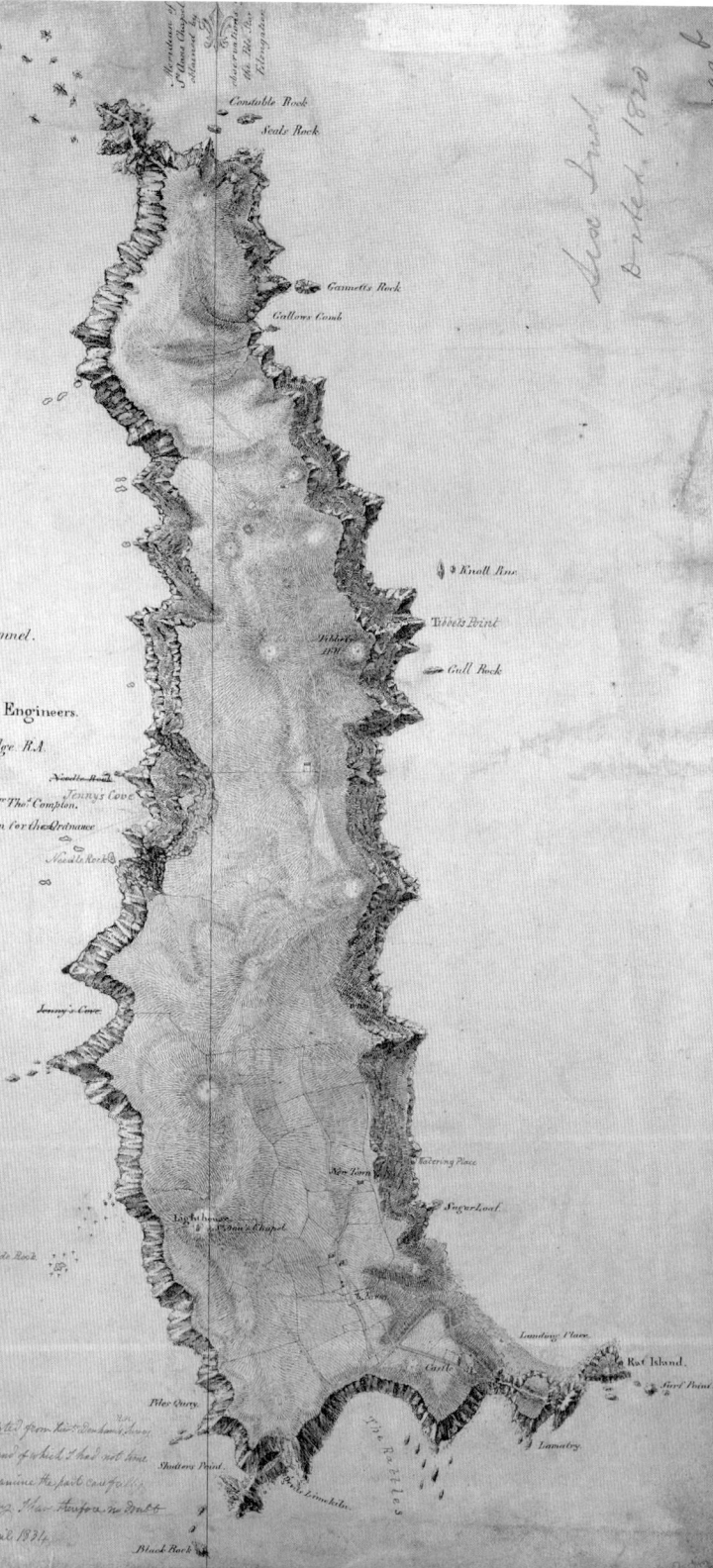

Lundy, a pirate island off the coast of Devon.

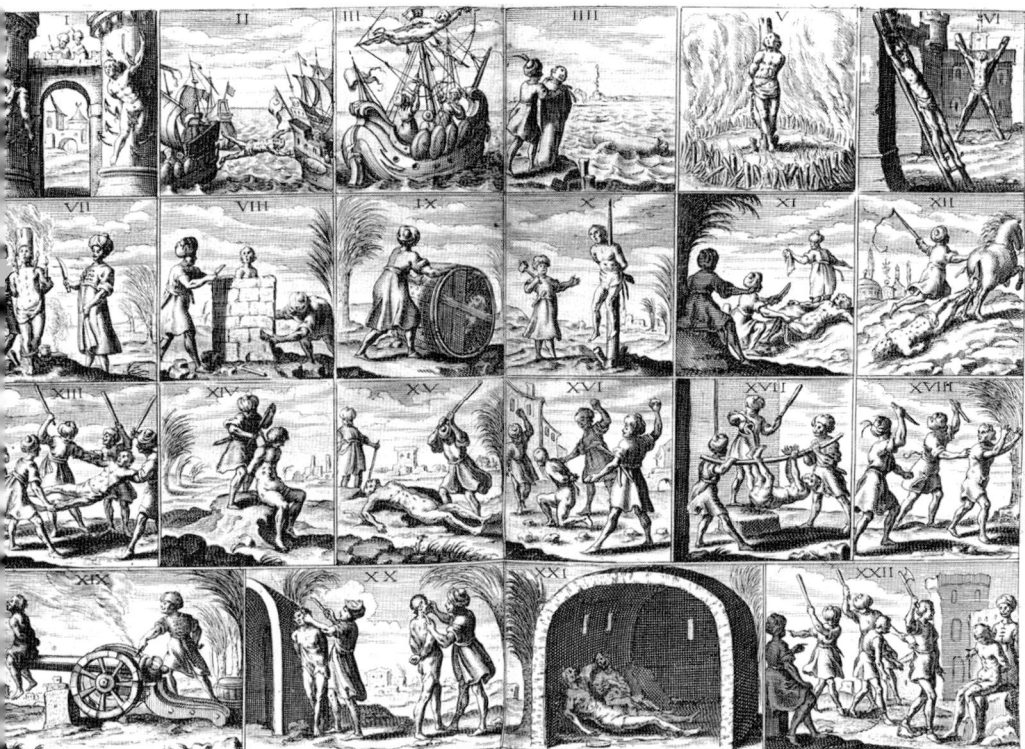
Examples of the tortures to which Christian slaves in North Africa were supposedly put.

Jean le Vacher about to be blown from a cannon in Algiers.

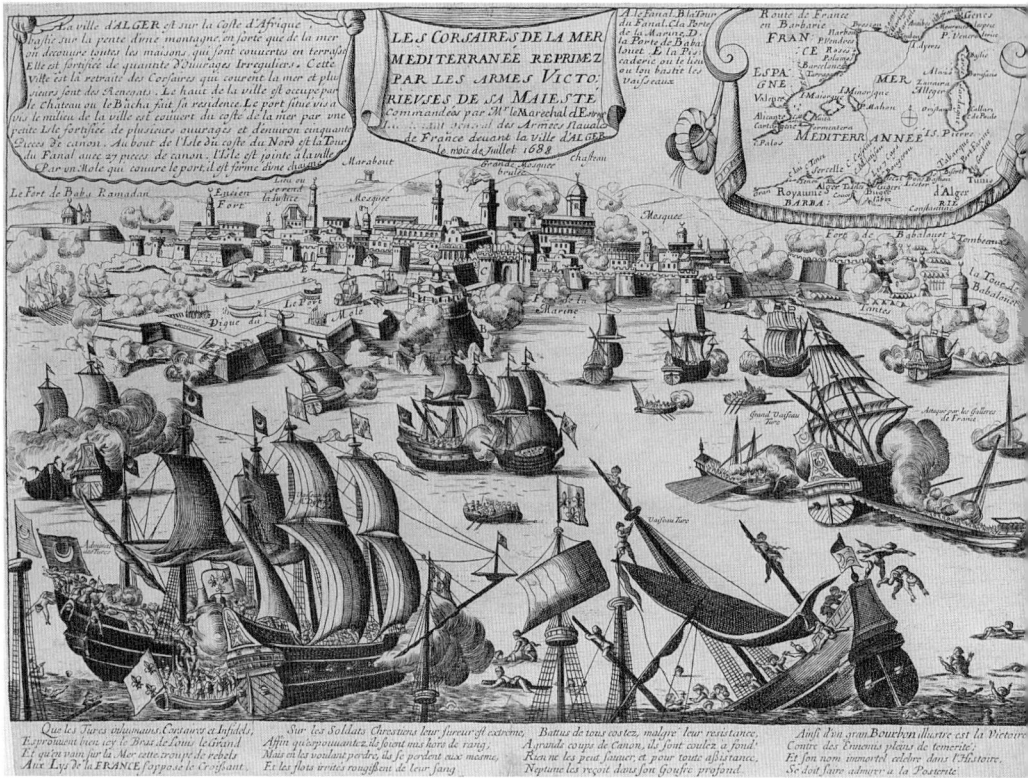

The French bombardment of Algiers in 1688.

Kara Mustafa Pasha being strangled with a silk cord.

Above left: Thomas Jefferson, who dealt firmly with the Barbary corsairs.

Above right: Commodore Barron of the *Chesapeake* surrenders to officers of the Royal Navy.

British sailors battling Barbary corsairs.

Above: The British bombardment of Algiers in the summer of 1816.

Left: European slaves in Algiers in 1816.

CAP.^T CROKER VISITING THE HOSPITAL AT ALGIERS.
A Mother informs him of the thirteen Years Slavery of herself and
her eight Children and points to six of them.   Page 6

CAP.^T CROKER HORROR STRICKEN AT ALGIERS,
on witnessing the Miseries of the Christian Slaves chaind & in Irons
driven home after labour by Infidels with large Whips.   Page 10111

CHRISTIAN SLAVERY AT ALGIERS.
1816.

Publishd by W. HONE, 55 Fleet Street,

Chapter 7

Fighting Back

Before and during the English Civil War, which lasted for almost a decade and finally ended in 1651, the privateers from the Barbary Coast more or less did as they pleased around the coasts of Britain. They seized ships and raided villages as the mood took them, taking people off into slavery. Charles I may well have had a strict policy of refusing to pay ransom, for fear of encouraging the taking of prisoners from land and sea, but he was too preoccupied with internal dissent in the country actually to do anything about the threat. Parliament took note of what was happening though.

Although a bitter civil war was being fought throughout the 1640s, the English Parliament still found time to consider the plight of English slaves held in North Africa. King Charles may have refused to send money to ransom captives, but Parliament was a little more sympathetic. The Civil War began in 1642 and on 25 April the following year Parliament passed the 'Ordinance for Collection to be made for relief of Captives in Algiers'. In 1644 came the 'Ordinance for the Redemption of Captives in Algiers' and then in 1645, the 'Ordinance for the raising of Moneys for the Redemption of distressed captives' (Firth & Rait, 1911). The aim of all these was to try and get together funds to pay for the ransom of English slaves who had been taken by the corsairs.

It was left to the man who succeeded Charles as ruler of the British Isles to tackle the problem in a determined and decisive way. Oliver Cromwell was not somebody to be trifled with and when he set out to take military action, it was usually successful. Some of his most ruthless and determined operations are still remembered with awe to this day. In Ireland the siege of Drogheda and subsequent massacre of the townsfolk remains a byword for barbarity.

One of the first steps which the Lord Protector of the Commonwealth, the title by which Cromwell became known, took to suppress what he saw as piracy was to reinstate the old means of execution for that crime. During the time of the Tudors, more imaginative methods of inflicting the death penalty were devised, which went beyond the simple hangings and decapitations to which people were accustomed, and typically included an element of poetic justice. Poisoners, who generally put their noxious substances into the food of their victims, were boiled alive as though they were themselves being cooked in a kitchen. Pirates, whose life was spent on the ocean, were punished by the sea itself, by being chained on the shore at low tide, so that they would be slowly drowned as the water came in (Kesselring, 2003). Cromwell revived this punishment, although the chances of actually taking prisoner and bringing to trial any of the corsairs roaming the English Channel and Irish Sea were slender in the extreme. That being so, the Lord Protector hit upon another scheme.

Although under Cromwell the navy in England was regaining some of its former strength, people were still being snatched from ships and seaside villages. Some of those who were caught were ferried across the Channel to France and then marched in long slave caravans across the country to the Mediterranean coast, where another slaver would collect them for the short trip across the Mediterranean to Algiers or Tunis. The eighteenth-century historian Thomas Carte summed up this route neatly, saying that the corsairs,

> carried their English captives to France, drove them in chains overland to Marseilles, to ship them thence with greater safety for slaves to Algiers. (Sumner, 1853)

Of course, not only did Oliver Cromwell have the greatest possible objection to seeing his country's citizens carried off in this way and he himself made to look foolish and ineffectual; he had another powerful reason for resenting the activities of the Barbary corsairs. He was a devout and deeply religious man; indeed, a large part of the English Civil War had been bound up with the different brands of Christianity to which the Puritans and Parliamentarians adhered. As a Christian, of a kind that we would probably today describe as a fundamentalist, Cromwell was bitterly opposed to what he called 'profane nations', that is to say countries which were outside Christendom and followed some religion different from his own. This compounded the offence of attacking a Christian nation like England and made him all the more determined to put an end to the raids. Far-fetched images were circulated in pamphlets and supposedly depicted the sufferings of Christians when once they had fallen into the hands of the heathens. Illustration 12 shows some of the torments to which Christian slaves were allegedly put.

Parliament had had more ships than the Royalists during the Civil War, because as we have seen, the ports, including London, almost invariably declared against the king. The Royalists did acquire ships, but these tended to be privateers, hired from individuals who hoped to make a profit from the war. After the end of the English Civil War, Cromwell enlarged and reformed what had been the Royal Navy and set in charge of it a man who would be the perfect candidate if one wished to look for somebody able to strike a blow against the Ottomans on their own territory.

Robert Blake is affectionately known as 'The Father of the Royal Navy', but he was middle-aged before he ever became involved with warfare at sea. At the beginning of the English Civil War he was a Member of Parliament and joined the Parliamentary army as a captain, when he was already in his forties. He was rapidly promoted and, at the age of 51, appointed General-at-Sea, a rank roughly equivalent to admiral. In this role, he first chased a group of privateers under the command of the Royalist commander Prince Rupert, first from Ireland, then to Portugal and ultimately into the Mediterranean. This was the first time that English naval power had been successfully deployed in the Mediterranean and it caused consternation in France and Spain (Trevelyan, 1942).

After routing the Royalist ships, Robert Blake set the navy on a rigorous footing and established a code by which it would in the future operate. These ordinances were published in 1652 as *The Laws of War and Ordinances of the Sea (Ordained and Established by the Parliament of the Commonwealth of England)*. That same year, Blake's navy fought a series of engagements with the Dutch and established the North Sea and English Channel as being under the domination of the newly-formed Commonwealth.

Many of the countries in Europe regarded Cromwell's regime as an illegitimate upstart among the nations and were tempted to shun the government which had achieved final power by cutting off their monarch's head. The Lord Protector, as he was now styled, wanted to show once and for all that his country was a strong one and here to stay. One means of achieving this would be to deal with the scourge which had been troubling so much of Europe for almost a century. He decided to send a fleet into the Mediterranean to tackle the Barbary corsairs in their home ports. This would demonstrate three important lessons to the world. First, it would show that England viewed the Mediterranean Sea as within its sphere of influence and that English vessels would ply the waters there as and when they pleased. Secondly, it showed that despite the recent civil war, England was a power to be reckoned with. Thirdly and finally, the Barbary corsairs, which had been preying on Christian countries for many years, would receive a sharp lesson. This would also send a clear message to the Ottomans that they would be held to account for the actions of ships sailing from ports nominally under their control.

That the ships sailing from Tunis and Algiers were not pirates, but essentially acting as supplementary naval vessels of the Ottomans in Constantinople, may been seen clearly when we look in detail at Blake's expedition to the Barbary Coast in 1655. The ostensible reason for sending a fleet into the Mediterranean on this occasion was that an English ship had been seized by corsairs sailing from Tunis and the crew sold into slavery. General-at-Sea Blake came to the Barbary Coast to demand the release of the ship and for the crew to be freed. When he arrived at Tunis, Blake found quite a few ships gathered there. Rather than being out on the open seas, seizing ships from Christian nations, the corsairs were now preparing to sail to the Dardanelles to help the Ottoman Empire in its struggle with the Venetians. In other words, rather than behaving like pirates, they were now about to take part in a naval battle in support of militant Islam. The sultan in Constantinople was hoping to press further into Europe on land and also to show his mastery of the Mediterranean. Little wonder that the Barbary corsairs were at times referred to as being part of the 'Marine Jihad'.

The Dardanelles, that narrow strait which connects the Black Sea and Sea of Marmara with the Aegean and Mediterranean, has been of great importance historically. The only maritime access which Istanbul, or Constantinople as it then was, has with the Mediterranean and the high seas which lie beyond the Straits of Gibraltar is via the Dardanelles, which are less than a mile wide at their narrowest point. During the Cold War, the Soviet Black Sea Fleet was stationed at Sevastopol and could only enter the Mediterranean via the Dardanelles. Of course, the Dardanelles were also of great strategic importance during the First World War, when the British and Australians landed troops at Gallipoli, with the intention of seizing control of the Dardanelles and sending a fleet through to capture Constantinople. This narrow waterway was also crucially important from a strategic point of view in the seventeenth century, when the Ottomans were at the height of their power and still hoping to invade and occupy Europe. Achieving this end meant not only having a strong land army, but also being able to dominate the Mediterranean. It was for this reason that free passage through the Dardanelles was needed, so that the Ottoman fleet could pass to and fro, asserting their authority along the coasts of southern Europe.

One struggle in which the Ottoman Empire was engaged was with the city-state of Venice, which was itself a seagoing power. At about the time that the English fleet commanded by Robert Blake was heading towards the Barbary Coast, the Venetians were cruising around the Aegean Sea, that part of the Mediterranean which separates Greece from Turkey, with the intention of attacking the Ottoman ships should they venture out from the Dardanelles. The ships at Tunis and Algiers were getting ready to sail in support of the main Ottoman fleet, which was due to leave Constantinople in May or June.

Blake arrived at Tunis on 8 February 1655 with sixteen ships and at once sent word to the Bey of Tunis, who ruled that part of the North African coast on behalf of the Ottomans, that he required the return of the ship which had been detained, together with the release of the crew and indemnities against any future such action on the part of men operating out of Tunis. The Bey refused to give any assurance or to free the crew. He was prepared to negotiate a future deal with England but was not willing to discuss past actions or offer any compensation for them. This was not good enough, but although he was authorized by Cromwell himself to go to war over the matter, Blake decided to give the Bey time to reconsider his position. For one thing, teaching Tunis a lesson would not be a walkover. The place where the corsair ships lay at harbour was called Porto Farina (modern-day Ghar-al-Melh), a few miles north of Tunis. Porto Farina was heavily fortified and guarded by a castle boasting twenty cannons and garrisoned by Tunisian troops. There were also shore batteries of heavy guns, which were also protected by fortifications.

Because they were running low on drinking water, Robert Blake left six of his ships to blockade the harbour, where nine enemy ships lay at anchor, and then went off to the port of Cagliari in Sardinia, where he was able to take on provisions, before returning to the Barbary Coast. It must by now have been plain to the English force that the Bey of Tunis felt himself to be in an impregnable position and in no mood to compromise. What neither he nor Robert Blake could have known was that history was about to be made and the rules of naval warfare rewritten, not in the parochial sense of a minor skirmish off the coast of Africa, but in a much wider and more general way, which would affect the nature of warfare in the future.

On 18 March, the main part of the English fleet returned to Tunis and found that far from being willing to accede to their demands, the Bey of Tunis had spent the last month reinforcing the fortifications at Porto Farina and sending more troops to the area. He rejected another warning sent by Robert Blake and clearly felt himself in a strong military position. On being rebuffed once more, the entire English fleet left the North African coast and sailed to Sicily. This was partly a feint, to persuade the Bey of Tunis that the English had given up their blockade as a hopeless cause, but also to take on more supplies. On 3 April, they returned to Port Farina and at dawn the following day, the assault began.

The English fleet divided into three squadrons. Captain Cobham, who commanded the *Newcastle* with 40 guns, led the lighter ships in a raid on the vessels of the corsairs which lay in the harbour, while the other two squadrons, one led by Robert Blake on board the *George*, launched a bombardment of the castle and the shore batteries. The ships under Cobham's command sent boats towards the Tunisian ships, with the intention of boarding them. The Tunisians promptly abandoned their ships and the English sailors swarmed onto them and set fire to all nine of them. While this was going on, Tunisian snipers maintained a steady rate of fire on the attackers. It was the muskets which were responsible for almost all the casualties which the English suffered that morning, rather than the heavy artillery in the fortified positions on shore.

By 8:00am, every one of the corsair ships was burning. The other two squadrons had in the meantime been firing broadsides against the castle and fortified guns on the shore. They were aided by the wind, which was blowing from the sea towards the shore, and made it impossible for the Tunisians to see the English ships clearly. When they were certain that all the Tunisian ships were utterly destroyed, Robert Blake gave the order to withdraw. The English had lost twenty-five men killed and some eighty wounded. The engagement was, however, a resounding success. The artillery of the Tunisians had been put out of action simply by firing on it from ships. This was the first time such a thing had been achieved. All previous such battles had needed parties of men to be landed in order to take out heavy guns on land. Quite unintentionally, Robert Blake had changed the rules of naval warfare.

By the time that the English arrived at their next destination, Algiers, word had reached the Dey there of the events at Porto Farina. He agreed at once to free all the English slaves under his rule, negotiating a price for them. Of course, the fleet could have opened fire on Algiers, as they had on the Tunisian port, but satisfying as this would have been, it would not have resulted in the release of the slaves, which was their primary purpose. Not only did they ransom all the English captives in Algiers, the English crew had a collection among themselves and also found the money to pay for the freedom of forty Dutchmen who had also been enslaved. Some other slaves were so desperate to escape that they swam out to the English ships, where they were welcomed aboard.

The English action showed that the Mediterranean was now part of the British sphere of influence, a situation which exists to this day. Even now, the British bases in Cyprus are sovereign British territory, legally as much a part of Britain as Southend or Cardiff. Not only was this demonstration of English naval strength very useful from an international point of view, it was helpful for Cromwell on the domestic front too. The British public have always had a weakness for brisk and successful naval expeditions. One thinks of the defeat of the Spanish Armada in 1588 and also the retaking of the Falkland Islands in 1982 following their seizure by Argentina. If such actions are accomplished swiftly and with little loss of life, they are very popular in Britain. Margaret Thatcher's popularity soared after the brief Falklands War and she had an electoral triumph the following year.

The bloody nose which Oliver Cromwell gave the Bey of Tunis was so well received in England that even one of his former opponents was moved to write extravagant poetry about the raid on the Barbary Coast. Edmund Waller, a Royalist MP who had tried as hard as he could to prevent Oliver Cromwell winning in the English Civil War, was forced into exile after the war ended. Later, he returned to his own country and was so impressed by Cromwell's actions, particularly the way in which he dealt with the Barbary corsairs, that in the same year as Robert Blake's triumph at Porto Farina he wrote a lengthy poem inspired by the events in the Mediterranean. His *A Panegyric to my Lord Protector* was published in 1655. Part of it reads as follows:

> Hither the oppressed shall henceforth resort, Justice to crave, and succour, at your court; And then your Highness, not for ours alone, But for the world's protector shall be known.

> Fame, swifter than your winged navy, flies Through every land that near the ocean lies, Sounding your name, and telling dreadful news To all that piracy and rapine use. (Chernaik, 1964)

The English attack on Tunis had far-reaching effects, although not altogether those which had been hoped for and expected when they set out on their punitive expedition. The loss of the nine ships at Porto Farina affected the outcome of the sea battle fought between the Ottomans and Venetians a few months later. This was the Battle of the Dardanelles, which was, in retrospect, of great geopolitical significance, being essentially part of a struggle for the future of Europe. On such engagements as the naval battles between Venice and the Ottomans would hinge the question of whether Christendom or Islam triumphed in Europe.

The Venetians had for some years been fighting the Ottomans for mastery of the island of Crete. As part of this campaign, the ships of Venice were, in the summer of 1655, lying in wait for the Ottoman fleet to leave Constantinople and sail through the Dardanelles and into the Aegean Sea. On 21 June, the Ottoman ships left the Dardanelles and found the Venetians waiting for them. It was a hard-fought battle in which another nine or ten ships on the side of the Ottomans might well have made all the difference between victory or defeat. As it was, the Venetian routed the Ottomans. Although Crete fell to the Ottomans, within 15 years Venice was ultimately victorious.

The Barbary States and their ships were thus part of a monumental struggle for the very soul of Europe. The Pope was urging Christians on to the defence of their lands, warning that Christianity itself was in peril. The spirit of the Crusades was invoked, making this in at least some sense a religious war. For the Ottomans, the case was even more clear cut; the ships of the Barbary Coast and their own fleet were part of a marine jihad, whose aim was nothing less than the conquest of Europe and the imposition of Islam upon it. The battles between the Barbary corsairs and European ships were thus a small part of a momentous battle for the preservation of Christian civilization.

The Ottoman Empire had not yet entered its long decline, which would last for 250 years and end with the First World War. In the mid-seventeenth century it was very far from being the 'sick man of Europe', as it was famously described during the Crimean War. On the contrary, it was still thrusting aggressively westwards, seeking to absorb even more of Europe; a trend which would culminate with the siege of Vienna in 1683.

We looked above at a forgotten poem from English history, one with which few modern readers are likely to be familiar. The same cannot be said for *Rule, Britannia!*. The song *Rule, Britannia!* is represented by many liberal and progressive people to be a militaristic and imperialist paean, glorying in the superiority of the British armed forces over those of other nations. Its singing on the Last Night of the Proms generates controversy for this reason, such bellicose patriotism being considered a little dated. This trumpeting abroad the fact that our ships can beat anybody else's seems hardly appropriate in an age which values peaceful cooperation among nations. It is often interpreted as a hymn to Britain's lost empire, an awful nostalgia for a vanished age which is best forgotten. The song, which was written in 1740, is nothing of the kind. It celebrates England's struggle to protect her coastal waters from the Muslim slavers who, in the seventeenth century, actually did rule the waves around Britain.

We have read in this chapter and the previous one of the risks to British people of being captured by corsairs and carried off to a life of slavery. We have seen too how that danger was first diminished and then altogether obviated by resolute military action. When James Thompson wrote the words of *Rule, Britannia!* in 1740, it was to celebrate the success of Britain in securing the safety of her citizens by protecting the waters surrounding their country. It had nothing at all to do with imperialism or the expansion of British influence. The original line, now altered a little, 'Britons never will be slaves', refers directly to the role of the revitalised navy in deterring foreign ships from enslaving the inhabitants of Britain. It is a hymn of thanksgiving, rather than a proclamation of aggressive nationalism.

Despite Cromwell's ferocity and willingness to inflict damage on the states of North Africa, the problem of English seamen being taken as slaves persisted for another 150 years. The lesson taught at Porto Farina was not as salutary as might have been hoped, because six years later, Samuel Pepys was writing in his diary of meeting men who had been slaves in Algiers. The casual way in which he discusses this makes it obvious that there was nothing in the slightest degree remarkable about the accounts which he heard in the pub one Friday lunchtime, on 8 February 1661:

> At the office all the morning. At noon to the Exchange to meet Mr. Warren the timber merchant, but could not meet with him. Here I met with many sea commanders, and among others Captain Cuttle, and Curtis, and Mootham, and I, went to the Fleece Tavern to drink; and there we spent till four o'clock, telling stories of Algiers, and the manner of the life of slaves there! And truly Captn. Mootham and Mr. Dawes (who have been both slaves there) did make me fully acquainted with their condition there: as, how they eat nothing but bread and water. At their redemption they pay so much for the water they drink at the public fountaynes, during their being slaves. How they are beat upon the soles of their feet and bellies at the liberty of their padron. How they are all, at night, called into their master's Bagnard; and there they lie. How the poorest men do use their slaves best. How some rogues do live well, if they do invent to bring their masters in so much a week by their industry or theft; and then they are put to no other work at all. And theft there is counted no great crime at all. (Pepys, 1661)

Fifteen years after Pepys spent an afternoon listening to the harrowing stories of what slavery in Algiers was like for the Europeans seized by Barbary corsairs, the problem was still acute enough for Charles II to despatch a squadron of ships to the Mediterranean under the command of Sir John Narborough. After negotiating a peace deal with Tunis, Sir John proceeded to Tripoli and, finding the ruler there not amenable to reason, his ships bombarded the city until the Bey saw reason. Like Robert Blake before him, Sir John Narborough also succeeded in burning the ships laying at harbour when he attacked Tripoli.

It was a peculiar situation in which the English and other European nations now found themselves. There was no doubt that England's Royal Navy was more than a match for anything which the Ottoman provinces of Algiers, Tunis or Tripoli could send against them. The English were able to sail to the Mediterranean and bombard the coast of North Africa as much as they wished, but still men were being seized and made into slaves. In the next chapter, we will see why this was and what solution was eventually found which dealt with the problem of the Barbary corsairs in a more or less satisfactory fashion for well over a century. We will see too how America was drawn into the business and ultimately ended the scourge of the slave trade in that part of the world once and for all, at least as far as Europeans were concerned.

We end this chapter by looking at another incident which shows with great clarity that some at least of the European nations were quite capable of dealing militarily with the threat posed by the Barbary States. Algiers was generally regarded as the most troublesome of the Ottoman provinces along the Mediterranean coast of Africa. Corsairs were routinely described as 'Algerine', even if their actual nationality was unknown. Algiers was of course for many years, right up to the 1960s in fact, incorporated into France itself and regarded as being an integral part of that country, as French as Paris. This state of affairs had its origins in what were known in the nineteenth century as the Barbary Wars, but in 1682 this was all over a century in the future.

After the British naval victories against the Ottoman provinces in 1655 and 1675, it was apparent that the naval power of Europe was sufficient to inflict heavy damage and almost certain defeat upon Tunis, Algiers and Tripoli. This did not serve to stop the attacks on shipping in the Mediterranean though, which continued more or less unabated. When some French ships were boarded and the crews, as usual, taken to be sold as slaves, the King of France, Louis XIV, ordered his navy to mount a retaliatory attack on Algiers, from which the corsairs had in this instance sailed.

There was no appetite at all for putting 'boots on the ground', as we say today. The expedition launched by France to punish Algiers hoped to rely upon bombing alone to achieve its end. This was a fairly new idea and other nations watched with interest to see what the result of this novel scheme would be. The French sent eleven ships of the line, traditional warships of the day, fifteen galleys and five 'bomb galiots'. These were a new type of ship, small vessels with large mortars mounted on them, designed to hurl heavy shells at the city of Algiers. By August 1682, the French forces were anchored near Algiers and battle was about to commence. Just as with Robert Blake's assault on Porto Farina from the sea, the bombardment of Algiers by the French was to open a new chapter in warfare, showing that it was perfectly possible to 'shock and awe' an enemy population without hazarding a single member of your armed forces.

As with any completely new method of waging war, it took a little while for the new weapon to be successfully deployed. The small ships bearing the bomb-hurling mortars needed to be secured by cables to other French vessels, so that they could be held in position and manoeuvred until their missiles had maximum effect upon the intended target. On 26 August, the range was perfectly adjusted and bombs began raining down upon the city and port of Algiers. The result was devastating, with buildings collapsing all across the city and people fleeing in terror. On the night of 30 August, the great mosque was crowded with those who felt that God might protect them if they sheltered in His house. Several bombs struck the building though, causing part of it to collapse, burying alive those huddled in fear (Booth, 1865).

There was, somewhat surprisingly, a French consul in Algiers during all this fighting, although he was later to meet a gruesome end. Jean Le Vacher was a Catholic missionary who had spent as good deal of time in the Barbary States, negotiating the ransoming and release of French slaves. He combined the role of missionary with that of consul, which in time of war could be a hazardous business. During an interlude in the French bombardment, Jean Le Vacher offered to mediate between the Dey of Algiers and the French attackers. These talks led nowhere, but both sides appeared to regard the aging missionary, he was at that time 63, as an honest broker. A year later, luck ran out for the missionary-cum-consul.

Because French slaves were still being held in Algiers, another naval force was despatched from France in July 1683 and once again began shelling the city. Infuriated at their helplessness in the face of such an attack, the Algerians decided to vent their anger upon those Frenchmen who were at their mercy, including Jean Le Vacher. Algiers had at that time the most powerful cannon in the whole of the Mediterranean. It had been constructed by a Venetian engineer in 1542 and weighed 12 tons. This gigantic piece of ordinance was named Baba Merzoug. The 23ft long gun had a range of three miles. The unfortunate French consul was taken to Baba Merzoug and pushed partly into the barrel; the cannon then being discharged with a load of shrapnel, blowing him to pieces. A contemporary print of this incident may be seen in Illustration 13. The Algerians found twenty-two other Frenchmen and tied them to the muzzles of other guns and killed them in the same way.

One would hardly believe it after this episode, but another man volunteered to become the French consul in Algiers. Five years later, there was another dispute between France and Algiers, another French fleet arrived and then started firing at Algiers. The new consul, who was called Piolle André, found himself being dragged to where Baba Merzoug was positioned and was then treated in exactly the same way as Jean Le Vacher had been. Following this incident, Baba Merzoug was given a nickname by the Algerians. They began referring to it as the 'Consular'. The 1688 bombardment of Algiers is shown in Illustration 14.

To place the events in Algiers during 1682, 1683 and 1688 in their historical context, this was the time when the Ottoman Empire was expanding to its greatest limit in terms of the area it covered. 1683 was a pivotal year for the future of the whole of Europe, for it was then that the Ottomans launched an all-out assault on Europe which could, had it been successful, have led to the replacement of Christianity with Islam across the entire continent. Since Algiers was, at least in theory, a province of the Ottoman Empire, this was certainly something of which the Dey would have been aware.

In 1526 Suleiman the Magnificent, most famous of all the Ottoman sultans, had invaded Hungary and extended his power into Central Europe. The Hapsburg Empire, whose capital was Vienna, fought against this encroachment over the next century and a half, with limited success. The Muslims controlled the whole of the Middle East, North Africa, parts of Russia and Ukraine and were now edging forward menacingly towards Europe. The Habsburgs were not universally liked in Europe and the Ottomans supported various factions which were resisting the rule of Leopold I, who was emperor at that time. This had the effect of weakening the opposition to a Muslim invasion, a house divided being proverbially unable to withstand an enemy.

Two weeks before Jean Le Vacher was blown from the mouth of a cannon in Algiers an enormous Ottoman army arrived at Vienna. It had long been the ambition of the Ottoman sultans to control Vienna; both for practical and ideological reasons. As a matter of *realpolitik*, holding Vienna would give Constantinople control of various trade routes across Eastern, Western and Southern Europe. On a more exalted level, the seizure of the capital of the Holy Roman Empire would, it was hoped, deal a devastating, perhaps even mortal, blow to Christianity in Europe. It was for this reason, rather than because of any great love which they had for the Habsburgs, that other European countries were determined to prevent the fall of Vienna and offered to come to Austria's aid.

There was another reason for the Ottoman Empire choosing that particular year for their advance into Europe and it is one which is relevant to the subject of the trade in slaves. We have seen that the corps of the Janissaries was begun as a unit composed of foreign slaves, drawn chiefly from the Balkans. We saw too that Grand Viziers of the sultan often came from the same region and that some of them too were former slaves. In 1683, these two trends clashed and one group of European slaves and descendants of slaves fell out with a similar group, with disastrous consequences for the empire.

In 1676, a new Grand Vizier was appointed by Sultan Mehmed IV. The sultan was a little wary of Grand Viziers, because his father, the previous sultan Ibrihim the Mad, had been deposed and then strangled at the instigation of his then Grand Vizier. Mehmed was determined not let the same fate befall him. The man he chose to be grand Vizier was an Albanian who took the title of Merzifonlu Kara Mustafa Pasha. This man had married into the Koprulu family, who had provided all the Grand Viziers for the last 30 years or so. They too were Albanians, who had been brought to Turkey as a result of the devshirme. It is to be hoped that all these difficult and unfamiliar names will not bewilder or confuse readers.

The Koprulu family were engaged in trying to reduce the power of the Janissaries and as part of this strategy had created various diversions abroad, with the aim of occupying the Janissaries with actual fighting, rather than have them sitting around intriguing against the throne in the coffee houses of Constantinople (Williams, 2006). Expeditions took place to the Ukraine and the outer edges of the empire, in an attempt to find ways both to keep the Janissaries busily engaged and also to curry favour with the sultan by adding to his already swollen and overstretched empire. The siege of Vienna was part of this move.

It really was an extraordinary situation for a Turkish sultan to find himself in. The man to occupy the throne before him had been strangled with a silk cord, the traditional means of inflicting death on noble or aristocratic victims. This had been done at the command of a foreign slave who was supposed to be his servant. Meanwhile, other foreign slaves and their children were virtually holding the sultanate to ransom by their demands. The Janissaries, whose unit had been founded to avoid intrigues and plotting by the army against the throne, had turned out to be the greatest conspirators and instigators of schemes to overthrow sultans that had ever been known.

The sultans who had succeeded Suleiman the Magnificent had all had their eyes on Vienna, but were in no particular hurry. For over 100 years they built roads through Hungary and repaired bridges, slowly but surely planning for the inevitable day when the forces of Islam would sweep through Hungary and take Vienna, signalling the end of Christian dominance in Europe. Finally, on 14 July 1683, an army over 100,000 strong arrived at the gates of the Habsburg capital. Just 15,000 soldiers defended the city and the Ottomans must have felt unbeatable. What they could not have known was that Leopold I, the Hapsburg emperor, had been engaged over the summer, ever since it became plain that the sultan in Constantinople was intent upon a new war of expansion, in making treaties and alliances with other powers in Christian Europe. Whatever differences they had previously had were put aside in the face of an existential threat to Christendom.

There seemed to be little point to the attackers in mounting a direct assault on the city, with all the resultant casualties. The defender in such cases always has the advantage, from a purely military perspective. Instead, the Ottoman forces settled down for a siege, intending to starve Vienna into submission. They dug trenches and defensive positions around Vienna and simply waited. The Austrians though were not about to fight this battle single-handedly. Although Vienna had been the most likely target for Ottoman aggression, it was by no means impossible that they would choose instead to attack Poland. After all, there were already Ottoman forces in Russia and the Ukraine. Poland had therefore that year signed a mutual assistance pact with the Hapsburgs, whereby if Poland was attacked, the Austrians would come to their aid and if it was Vienna which was struck, then the Polish army would ride to the rescue. The stage was now set for a monumental clash of civilizations, as the Christian West prepared to fight with the Muslim East to decide the fate of Europe.

Vienna was protected by stout city walls and had more artillery than the attackers. The siege was thus likely to be a long and protracted one. By the end of August, food had run out in the city and the situation was desperate. The attacking Muslims were digging tunnels beneath the city walls, with a view to setting off large charges of gunpowder and so breaching the defences. This they managed to do and it looked as though it could only be a matter of time before Vienna fell and the Holy Roman Empire was, at a stroke, deprived of both its capital and its emperor. It was at this critical time that the forces of the King of Poland arrived.

Vienna was surrounded by now with some 140,000 enemy soldiers and the army of Germans, Austrians and Poles which arrived to relieve the siege numbered barely half that. At 4:00am on 11 September 1683, battle was joined. The Ottomans were a little dispirited by this time. They had, after all, been sitting before the walls of Vienna for almost two months and their efforts to bring down the walls had met with only limited success. The fighting was fierce and lasted for 12 hours, until the Polish army delivered the death blow. They had held in reserve no fewer than 18,000 mounted men and at 4:00pm this huge body of men swept down from the hills upon the Ottoman forces. It was by far the biggest cavalry charge in history and proved decisive. The Ottoman army was comprehensively defeated. In 1683, the Ottoman Empire reached its greatest extent and after the failed siege of Vienna was destined slowly to shrink in size. Europe was saved.

The Grand Vizier had accompanied the army himself, hoping that the glory of being present when Vienna fell would ensure his place among the greatest heroes of the empire. His camp was incredibly lavish and showed that even when he was on a military campaign, Merzifonlu Kara Mustafa Pasha had no intention of allowing his standards to slip. After the siege was lifted and the Ottomans driven back, the King of Poland, Jan Sobieski, wrote to his wife about what had been found after the battle. The Grand Vizier had tried to destroy any of his belongings, rather than let them fall into the hands of the enemy. For reasons at which we can only guess, he had taken with him to war a pet ostrich and Sobieski wrote, 'The Vizier had a marvellously beautiful ostrich – but this too he had killed . . . ' Not only ostriches had been included among the items which Kara Mustafa Pasha had brought with him to the battlefield. Jan Sobieski's letter continued that the Grand Vizier 'had baths; he had gardens and fountains; rabbits and cats, and a parrot which kept flying about so that we could not catch it.' Retribution was swift to fall upon Kara Mustafa Pasha for the loss of face which the sultan suffered after the terrible defeat at Vienna. When the retreating army reached Belgrade, orders were sent that the Grand Vizier was to be disposed of at once. Just like the sultan's father, he was strangled with a silk cord, a process which may be seen in Illustration 15.

It has been remarked earlier that without a proper understanding of the slave trade in which the Ottomans and their allies engaged, it is impossible to make sense of a lot of history. Here is another example. If Vienna had fallen to the Turkish army, then the rest of Europe might have been gradually encroached upon, until Islam replaced Christianity as the dominant religion. The entire enterprise, which could easily have succeeded, was begun by one slave in order to tackle the problems caused by another group of slaves. On this hung the fate of Christian Europe.

The effects of these events linger on to this day. When, in 2015, a column of refugees, many of them Muslims, were tramping north through the Balkans and across Hungary, memories of the past were evoked. The seemingly endless lines of tramping men originated from Turkey and were predominantly Muslim. It would have been difficult for anybody in Hungary, which had once been an Ottoman vassal state, not to remember previous invasions and to view this mass movement in a similar light. Western Europe, which had never been menaced by the Ottomans, failed to understand the visceral reaction to the sight of a column of Muslim men marching through the Balkans from Turkey and denounced any uneasiness felt in that region as being motivated by Islamophobia or hatred of refugees.

Returning now to the matter of Algiers, France was not the only European power to fight a war against Algiers at this time. The Netherlands were at war with the Barbary state almost continuously for more than a century from 1618 to 1726. There were periods when a state of war did not technically exist, but these did not last. Between 1618 and 1622, 1630 and 1662, from 1664 to 1679, 1686 to 1712 and from 1715 to 1726 The Netherlands was at war with Algiers. It might be wondered why a northern European country like The Netherlands cared so much about being able to send its ships into the Mediterranean, but the answer is very simple.

Trade between northern and southern Europe was enormously profitable during the seventeenth, eighteenth and nineteenth centuries and the prosperity of The Netherlands was founded upon this commerce. Of course, carrying large quantities of goods by wagon train across Europe, through the Alps to Italy and so on, would be an arduous, time-consuming and expensive process. It was far easier to load up a ship and then simply sail south, through the Straits of Gibraltar and then to Italy. Once in the Mediterranean, once could then also travel on to Alexandria in Egypt or even along the Dardanelles to Constantinople. There was of course a fly in the ointment; a very large fly in the form of the Barbary corsairs, who knew how profitable this traffic in goods was and wanted a share of the business without actually doing anything to earn it. Ships could, and did, travel in convoys for safety, but this was a cumbersome and awkward proceeding. Various European nations tried to bully and bluff states like Algiers into reining in the corsairs, but this only ever provided a short-term solution. If the prosperity of Europe depended upon trade, then the prosperity of the Barbary Coast relied upon preying on that trade and extracting a share of it. During the eighteenth century an accommodation was reached between European sea-powers and the Barbary States, one which was, on the whole, agreeable to both parties.

Chapter 8

Paying the Dane-Geld

We arrive now at what is at first sight something of a conundrum. By the end of the seventeenth century it was obvious that European nations like England and France were well able to defeat the Barbary States militarily and even, if they wished to do so, overthrow their governments and occupy their territory. That they did not do so when it was within their power is a little puzzling. Instead of crushing them and reducing their countries to nothing, England arranged to pay 'tribute' to the rulers of Algiers and the neighbouring provinces, which almost sounds as though it was England which had been defeated and forced into humiliating submission. This tribute was paid for over a century.

The relations of the great European powers of England, France, Holland and Spain with the Barbary States was governed strictly by *realpolitik* and once this is understood, everything falls into place. Military adventures are costly and usually avoided by prudent nations whenever possible without too much loss of face. The occasional victory on the battlefield or at sea is heartening and popular with ordinary people, but they do not want their standard of living to be reduced by constant wars and petty conflicts. Burning the corsair ships of Tunis in 1655 played very well to a domestic audience in Britain at that time, to give one example, but most citizens of Cromwell's Commonwealth wanted to see food on their tables, rather than news of glorious victories a thousand miles away.

However, we know that the British Empire was beginning to grow in the eighteenth century. Wars of conquest were being fought in various places and invasions launched. Why wasn't the British army simply sent to North Africa and ordered to invade and occupy Algiers and add it to the various other overseas possessions of the nascent empire?

The reason is simple. The British Empire grew by acquiring territory or colonies which would benefit and enrich the citizens of Britain. From America and the Caribbean came sugar and tobacco, India provided woven textiles, the Far East sent spices, Equatorial Africa sent ivory. This was the whole purpose of imperialism, taking over and colonizing the land of others, so that Britain would benefit. From this perspective, there would have been little advantage to seizing North Africa. There were no natural resources, nothing to exploit and, worst of all, it would put Britain on a collision course with the Ottoman Empire, of which the Barbary States were, at least nominally, provinces.

Then too, it will be recalled that although Robert Blake had beaten Tunis by destroying their castle and burning their ships, this had not caused them to free their English slaves. All the English slaves in Algiers had been freed a short while later though, by the simple expedient of exchanging them for gold. The French bombardment of Algiers had been a glorious victory, but had also resulted in the murder of French people living in that city, not their being freed and allowed to return to France.

In short, military actions were very expensive and largely pointless if your aim was actually to effect the release of captives. The way to do that was by paying in cash. Looked at from a strictly economic viewpoint, there was no contest; ransoming was the surest and most inexpensive means of restoring their liberty. Of course, if you could simply hand over the money beforehand, and by paying in advance, as it were, prevent the taking of ships and their crews in the first place, that would be even better.

There was one final factor which encouraged the British, French, Spanish and Dutch to tolerate the Barbary corsairs throughout the eighteenth century. By paying tribute, those wealthy nations could avoid the inconvenience and expense of having their ships molested in the first place. Smaller nations, though, might not be able to afford to pay off those running what amounted to a protection racket. Belgian or Danish ships were regarded as fair game and this reduced the competition which British traders faced as they operated in the Mediterranean.

In this way, the wealthier and more commercially important nations were able to use the Barbary corsairs to discourage other countries from sending merchant shipping into the Mediterranean.

The wisdom of the British policy in this matter was beautifully illustrated by the course of the Danish-Algerian War of 1769–72. This is perhaps a conflict of which scarcely anybody today has heard, even those living in Denmark. It showed how shrewdly the British had played their hand in the matter of Mediterranean trade.

From the middle of the sixteenth century until 1814, Denmark and Norway were one, unified realm. Denmark-Norway was a colonial power, with overseas possessions in India, Africa and the Caribbean. Who today remembers the Danish West Indies? At its height, this empire covered more than a million square miles. Denmark-Norway traded around the world and their ships plied the Atlantic and Indian Oceans, as well as passing regularly across the Mediterranean. Because the country was looking prosperous and able to pay hefty ransoms, the Barbary corsairs began targeting Danish ships. There had already been raids on Danish dependencies in the North Atlantic, we looked in an earlier chapter at the raid on Iceland in the seventeenth century. The Faroe Islands were also attacked. As Danish trade increased, the corsairs began to feel that such a thriving country would be able to pay handsomely for the release of slaves.

In June 1706 a Danish warship, the *St Christopher*, was attacked after she left the Italian port of Livorno. The crew of forty were taken to Algiers and sold as slaves. The King of Denmark arranged for the officers and some of the ordinary seamen to be ransomed, but eight years later some of the sailors from the *St Christopher* were still slaves. Two years after the capture of the *St Christopher* another Danish ship, the *Fortuna*, was taken by Algerian ships and the crew ended up in a slave market. It seemed to Denmark-Norway that the best way of protecting their ships was to enter into the same kind of arrangement with Algeria as that which had been made with Britain. This was duly done and the Danes agreed to pay a certain amount of tribute regularly, in order to secure immunity for their vessels as they sailed across the Mediterranean or passed through the Atlantic near Portugal and Spain. For some years, this deal was observed.

We observe in passing that there is something rather sad about the Danes being reduced to such a position. It was from Denmark of course that the Vikings emerged as a fearsome power in the Middle Ages and at one time they were a byword in terror from Moscow to North America. Now, they were having to haggle with the statelets of the North African coast and plead for their ships to be let alone. Those marauding Vikings of old must have been turning in their graves at such a reversal of fortune!

It was of course one thing for a militarily strong country like Britain or France to enter into a financial arrangement with Algiers from a position of strength, but Denmark-Norway was not a particularly powerful nation from that point of view. That being so, there was always a temptation on the part of those running this international racket to try and change the terms of the deal they had struck and demand more money. There are many precedents for this kind of situation, a good and incidentally most apposite one being the paying of the Dane-Geld by the Anglo-Saxons in the late tenth and early eleventh centuries. This was also known as 'tribute' and any student of history who is minded to pay 'tribute' or ransom would be well-advised to consider what happened in that case.

The Danes were fierce plunderers who saw England, to use a modern idiom, as a soft touch. They landed and threatened to wreak havoc and take what they pleased. Of course, if the English wished to avoid fighting and looting, then they could simply hand over a cash settlement and the Danes would return peacefully to their own country. As Rudyard Kipling put it so succinctly in his poem *Dane-Geld*;

It is always a temptation to a rich and lazy nation,
To puff and look important and to say:-
'Though we know we should defeat you, we have not the time to meet you,
We will therefore pay you cash to go away'. (Kipling, 1911)

The problem with that approach is that once you have paid up, there are likely to be increasingly outrageous demands for more and more money. In the case of the Dane-Geld which England paid to avoid trouble, this eventually amounted to over 60 million silver pennies. So much money was handed over that more English pennies of that period have been found in Denmark than in England where they were minted. History, as well as common sense, tell us that paying a blackmailer or somebody running a protection racket will inevitably result in demands for further and greater sums of money, if once we give in.

There is an amusing irony in that the Danes, having extracted tribute in this way themselves should, 800 years later, fall prey to the same trick. Nevertheless, that is exactly what happened in 1766 when Baba Mohammed ben-Osman became the new Dey of Algiers. Not only did he increase the protection money which Denmark-Norway would have to pay each year, he also demanded some personal gifts to mark his accession to power. The Danes refused to have their treaty unilaterally amended in this way and effectively told the Dey that he would not be getting any presents or increase in the annual fees which were already being paid. The Algerian response was predictable; three Danish ships were captured at sea and the crews all sold into slavery.

Now if you are going to adopt a tough line in matters of this kind, then you really should do it before you hand over any money. This is what the British did, proving first to the Barbary States that Britain was able and willing to launch punitive raids on their cities should the need arise. Only after showing their teeth did the British agree terms for tribute. The Danes followed precisely the opposite path; paying first and then cutting up rough later. This did not bode well for them.

On 16 May 1770 a number of warships were despatched from Copenhagen, the Danish capital. It was, to say the least of it, a very small armada, consisting of just four ships of the line, accompanied by two frigates and two bomb galiots of the kind which the French had used with great success a century earlier. They sailed to Algiers, where a message was sent to the new Dey, threatening to bombard the city unless the Danish and Norwegian sailors who had been sold us slaves were released and allowed to return to their own countries. The Dey was unimpressed and more or less told the Danes to do their worst (Ødegaard, 2010).

Of course, if you are hoping to menace any potential adversary with force, then it is essential to make sure that you are in a strong enough position to inflict substantial harm should your threats prove unavailing. This was not at all the case with the Danish taskforce. The six warships and two mortar-carrying Galiots did not really pose a credible threat to Algiers. Indeed, having learned the lessons of the French attacks of the 1680s, the Algerians had developed their own defensive system which was about to be put to the test.

The Danish expedition suffered two blows during their supposed siege of Algiers. The first was a terrible outbreak of typhoid, which is spread by contaminated water. This caused the death of hundreds of sailors. The second setback was even worse. Having been rebuffed in their negotiations, the Danes decided to take a tough and uncompromising line, shelling Algiers with their sea-borne mortars. It was a dreadful miscalculation on their part, because the Algerians had had a century to prepare for an attack of this kind since it had proved so successful when used by the French. They had constructed mortars of their own, which allowed them to hurl bombs back at the attacking ships. The Danish-Norwegian force was able to send seventy-five shells into the port of Algiers, before they were compelled to break off the attack and withdraw. Their ships were being damaged by the explosions which the Algerian weapons were causing and had they remained in position, then the six ships would inevitably have been sunk.

Algiers and Denmark had reached an impasse. The Danish fleet was so weakened by disease that they were unable to continue an assault on a heavily-defended city and had been forced to withdraw. Their ships though were more powerful and better armed than those of Algiers and so would probably defeat them in a battle at sea. The Danish forces therefore imposed a blockade upon the city, refusing as far as possible to let any ships enter or leave the port. This standoff lingered on and it became increasingly obvious that Algiers was not going to change its attitude. The Dey was perfectly prepared to wait until the Danish forces had had enough of it, which of course eventually happened. Maintaining a naval blockade for months or years at a time is a huge drain on a country's resources and back in Copenhagen the government was becoming restless about the expense and eventually decided that paying an increased amount of tribute might not be so burdensome as keeping their fleet standing idle far from home, essentially doing nothing for months on end.

In 1772, two years after the Danish-Norwegian ships had arrived in the Mediterranean to teach Algiers a stiff lesson, a delegation was sent to the Dey of Algiers and agreed to the increased tribute which had been the cause of all the trouble in the first place. It was a humiliating climbdown, made worse by the fact that during the fighting in 1770, some of the sailors in the attacking force had fallen into Algerian hands and promptly been sold as slaves. Their freedom had to be negotiated and those who had bought them as slaves adequately recompensed.

The events of the Danish-Algerian War suggested to some European nations that the system of tribute actually worked and was really a lot less trouble than fighting wars to maintain the free passage of merchant vessels through the Mediterranean. Even so, further attempts were made to curb Algerian attacks on shipping as the eighteenth century drew to a close, most notably by the Spanish in 1775.

Spain had preceded other nations in Europe in seeing the Barbary Coast as being an area suitable for colonial expansion. The Spanish had a fort at Melilla, in Morocco, which they had defended successfully against a Moroccan siege in 1774 and the following year thought that it might be time to show what a modern European army could do when directed by determined leaders. The whole of Europe had found Algiers to be a nuisance for the better part of 200 years and all attempts to put a stop to the corsairs operating out of the port had come to nothing. Ships were still being captured and their crews taken to the slave market in Algiers and the most recent attempt to bring the Dey of Algiers to heel, that made by the Danish-Norwegian force, had ended ignominiously. It was time for Spain to show what could be done. It would provide a marvellous demonstration too, to the sultan of Morocco, that Spain was going to do as it pleased in North Africa and that if the Moroccans were not careful, then they would be dealt with in the same ferocious way as Algiers. So much for the theory behind the Spanish expedition. It bore little resemblance to the actual course of events as they unfolded in July 1775.

On paper, the army which Charles III of Spain sent to conquer Algiers looked formidable, one might almost be tempted to say invincible. A total of 20,000 men under arms carried in a vast armada. In addition to seven ships of the line, there were twelve frigates, twenty-seven gunboats and a dozen other warships, including four mortar-boats. There were also over 200 other vessels to carry troops ashore (Jaques, 2006). With such immense military power, what could possibly go wrong? In fact, things began to go wrong as soon as the landings commenced.

The Spanish troops were used to operating on springy turf and hard, dry and dusty roads, rather than the conditions they actually encountered at the beach-heads. No sooner was the heavy artillery hauled ashore than it sank into the soft sand and remained stuck there, immovable. Because there were so many of them and they were so heavily armed, the Spanish army was over-confident to the point of recklessness. What they did not know was that Berber merchants in France had been receiving information about the Spanish force before they even embarked for Algiers. Preparations had therefore been carefully laid long before the Spanish appeared off the coast.

A fairly small and lightly armed force of Algerians made a feint of attacking the Spanish as they landed and then, when a counter-attack was launched, these men swiftly retreated. Victory seemed to be within easy grasp and the invaders hastened after the apparently fleeing enemy. Too late, they found themselves in a deadly trap. The wild Berbers from the interior might have had no particular love for the Dey of Algiers but seeing a European army land to occupy their territory was not something with which they were prepared to put up. A force equal in number to that fielded by the Spanish was waiting behind the sand dunes and these men swept down upon the amazed soldiers who, a few minutes earlier had believed that they could invade and occupy somebody else's country with no difficulty at all. Surrounded by hostile forces, the Spanish began withdrawing to the beach, desperate to board their ships and landing craft to escape the fierce Berbers and Arabs who were now driving them back in a complete rout.

The Spanish casualties were heavy and included no fewer than five generals who were killed and another fifteen who were wounded. After the survivors of the exquisitely-organized ambush were safely aboard their ships, there was some talk of bombarding Algiers in reprisal, but even that was impossible. There were not enough provisions to last any longer than the time it would take to sail straight back to Spain. So confident of success had been those organizing this bloody fiasco that they had only loaded enough food and water for a one-way trip from Spain to Algiers, assuming that once they had taken Algiers, they would be able to live off the resources in the city.

Flushed with their success against Spain, the Algerians believed themselves invulnerable and their corsairs continued to roam the Mediterranean, taking slaves pretty much as they pleased. The days of such freedom though were coming to an end, although this may only be seen in retrospect. With the Industrial Revolution gathering pace in Europe, it was absurd to think that pirates and corsairs were still prowling the shores of southern Europe and demanding protection money. Eight years after they had been driven from Algiers, the Spanish returned. The actions of the corsairs were once again becoming an intolerable nuisance and it was time to call a halt to them. In 1783 a Spanish fleet again sailed for Algiers. This time there was no question of landing. The intention was to deliver a punishing blow to the city by pummelling it with artillery from the sea. This was done for eight days in August, causing significant damage to the city and port. The Dey refused to discuss terms and the Spanish ships returned home, believing that they had given a salutary warning of what the Algerians could expect if they did not mend their ways and stop interfering with shipping. A month later, they found that they were quite mistaken.

In September 1783 two Spanish merchant ships were sailing past Palamós, a town on that part of the Spanish coast which is now known as the Costa Brava. Five Algerian privateers attacked and captured both ships, the crew being taken to sell into slavery. This was Algiers' response to the events that summer. The message was plain; the Barbary corsairs were still in business.

One big difference about the world 250 years ago is that things happened in those days at a much more leisurely pace than is now the case. Sending messages by ship and waiting for a reply could take weeks or months and travel depended heavily upon the weather and the season. So it was that despite the insolent and provocative actions of the Algerians, effectively thumbing their nose at Spain and showing that the attack on their city had made no difference at all to the way in which they proposed to behave, it was almost a year before Algiers received Spain's response to the taking of their ships so close to the Spanish coast.

Fighting wars at sea in the winter is an unpredictable enterprise and you are as likely to be shipwrecked as you are to suffer at the hands of the enemy's cannons. For this reason, the next attack on Algiers did not take place immediately but was delayed until the following summer. Such things took time to plan as well, with letters to be sent, supplies ordered and so on. In this particular case, arrangements for the reprisal against the corsairs of the Barbary Coast took even longer, because the Spanish wanted to find allies who would join in the venture and also, if possible, somebody who would finance the whole thing. As it chanced, Pope Pius VI was keen to see the Ottoman Turks given a bloody nose, to show that Christendom could still give the Caliphate a run for its money. Two other nations were keen to join Spain in dealing what it was hoped would be a knockout blow to Algiers. The Kingdom of Sicily had suffered at the hands of the corsairs, as had Malta. Both were very keen to take the Dey of Algiers down a peg or two.

If the Spanish were able to find allies, so too were the Algerians. It must be remembered that Algiers was still a province of the Ottoman

Empire and that it would be a blow to the Ottomans if one of their cities were to be destroyed or captured by the Christians. For this reason, thousands of Turkish soldiers came to Algiers to help repulse any attack by Spain. New fortifications were constructed, including a fortress boasting no fewer than fifty guns. The Dey was sure that he and his city could withstand anything thrown at it.

The allied European fleet set off from the Spanish port of Cartagena on 29 June 1784. On 10 July they reached Algiers, where they anchored. Then, on the morning 12 July, an enormous barrage was unleashed against the town. During that first day, between 8:30am and 4:20pm that same afternoon, a total of 1,440 cannonballs, 600 bombs and 200 shells were fired at the city. The Algerian response was lively, but with considerably less firepower at their disposal, they could not hope to defend themselves effectively against this mighty onslaught. The next day, the bombardment was resumed and continued for eight successive days. At the end of this time, more than 20,000 cannon-balls and bombs had been fired at Algiers, causing widespread devastation. It was obvious that the Spanish had the ability to inflict as much damage as they wished.

It looked to everybody in both Europe and the Barbary Coast that the Spanish attack on Algiers in 1784 marked the end of the days of the corsairs and slavers having a free rein in the Mediterranean. The leader of the Spanish expedition sent word to the Dey of Algiers that he was already planning a new assault and that his government had authorized attacks every year on Algiers, until they freed slaves and put an end to the activities of the corsairs. The prospect of facing such annual destruction was too much for the Dey and he agreed to sign a treaty with Spain. Tunis, seeing which way the wind was blowing, also offered without any prompting to sign a similar agreement that they would stop anybody sailing from their shores to seize ships or slaves. At long last, or so it appeared, the problem of the Barbary corsairs had been dealt with once and for all.

There was to be a coda to the centuries-long struggle against the slavers and privateers from the Barbary Coast and it was in the end not a European nation at all which took the military actions which ended the brigandry of the Ottoman provinces, but the new nation of America. We shall look at the resurgence of corsair activity in the North Atlantic and Mediterranean oceans in Chapter 10, but before doing so it is time to turn to Morocco and see what was happening there during the period we have so far examined. Morocco was an independent kingdom and not a province of the Ottoman Empire and so the situation was different from that in Algiers, Tunis and Tripoli.

Chapter 9

The Salé Rovers

From the late seventeenth century onwards, the Ottoman Empire was in retreat. It had been transformed by various factors from a vigorous and energetic entity, thrusting forward into Europe and actually threatening to take over that continent, into a shadow of its former self. Before looking in more detail at the decline of Turkey and its empire and its transformation into the 'sick man' of Europe, we might turn to one part of the Barbary Coast at which we have not yet looked in detail. This is Morocco and the Republic of Salé, a short-lived city-state which for a few decades flourished as a sister-city to Rabat, the present-day capital of Morocco. Salé was heavily involved in the Barbary slave trade and although the name is unlikely to be immediately recognized by English readers today, it was once familiar to any literate and well-read person.

We saw that Cervantes, author of *Don Quixote*, spent some years as a slave in Africa. His famous novel mentions slavery in several contexts. One incident occurs when Don Quixote frees some galley slaves and there are references to black African slaves as well. There are several contenders for the first English novel, but *Robinson Crusoe* by Daniel Defoe, published in 1719, is frequently cited as the most generally accepted candidate for this title. In recent years, *Robinson Crusoe* has fallen from popularity and is nowhere nearly as widely read as it once was. Most people are aware that it concerns a shipwrecked sailor on a desert island and have heard of 'Man Friday' though, even if they have not actually read the book. What may come as a surprise is that the plot of *Robinson Crusoe* is heavily bound up with slavery, including that practised by the Barbary corsairs.

Early on in *Robinson Crusoe*, the eponymous protagonist decides to become a slave trader and signs on a slaving ship headed for Guinea, to transport African slaves across the Atlantic. Perhaps it rather serves him right when *en route* to Africa, the ship he is sailing on is attacked by what is described as 'Sallee rovers'. These are in fact Barbary corsairs from what is now Morocco. There is an exciting sea battle which culminates in Crusoe's capture;

> However, to cut short this melancholy part of our story, our ship being disabled, and three of our men killed, and eight wounded, we were obliged to yield, and were carried all prisoners into Sallee, a port belonging to the Moors. The usage I had there was not so dreadful as at first I apprehended; nor was I carried up the country to the emperor's court, as the rest of our men were, but was kept by the captain of the rover as his proper prize, and made his slave, being young and nimble, and fit for his business. At this surprising change of my circumstances, from a merchant to a miserable slave, I was perfectly overwhelmed; and now I looked back upon my father's prophetic discourse to me, that I should be miserable and have none to relieve me, which I thought was now so effectually brought to pass that I could not be worse; for now the hand of Heaven had overtaken me, and I was undone without redemption; but, alas! this was but a taste of the misery I was to go through, as will appear in the sequel of this story. (Defoe, 1719)

It is little wonder that many readers, when first this book was published, believed it to be a genuine, autobiographical account. There can be no doubt that Daniel Defoe must have interviewed some sailors who had been taken in this way, because he goes on to give a very detailed account of the two years which Robinson Crusoe spent as a slave in Morocco. Crusoe's spell as a slave does not appear to teach him anything, because as soon as he manages to escape, he once again becomes mixed up with the trade in black Africans who are being taken across the Atlantic Ocean.

Where and what was 'Sallee', about which Defoe wrote? At the end of the fifteenth century, the Spanish had regained control of the whole of the Iberian Peninsula and the realm of Grenada came to an end. A few years later, Islam was outlawed in the country and Arabs and those of Arab descent in Spain were obliged either to leave the country or convert to Christianity. For a century or so, these people, known as Moriscos, were tolerated, but then the decision was made to expel them from Spain, just as Jews had earlier been ejected from the country. Shortly before this edict was promulgated, a group of 3,000 or so Moriscos left Spain and set up a base near the Moroccan city of Rabat. Morocco was an independent kingdom at that time, rather than being a part of the Ottoman Empire. However, it was in a parlous state, with a civil war brewing. The Arab dynasty which controlled Morocco had a tenuous grip upon parts of the kingdom. The Moriscos who settled near Rabat were fairly well-to-do, but they were joined after 1619 by 10,000 other Moriscos who had been ejected from Spain under the expulsion edicts. These people were less prosperous; many of them were penniless refugees. For want of any other occupations, this expatriate community decided that preying on shipping which was heading past Africa, to or from India or the Far East, or into the Mediterranean, might provide them with a good living.

The Sultan of Morocco allowed the settlement of Salé to establish itself near his own capital not only because he was struggling to maintain his rule, but also because he could see that this was likely to prove a profitable business. He arranged with the men of Salé that they would pay him 10 per cent of their earnings, either in slaves or treasure. So it was that the Republic of Salé was founded, a separate little enclave within Moroccan territory. Another thread in the history of the Barbary corsairs had begun.

Salé could hardly have been better situated to prey on European shipping. It was only a couple of hundred miles from the Straits of Gibraltar, which meant that its ships could prowl the seas in the vicinity of the straits and pounce on any likely victim. It was also on the African coast and ships sailing to India or the Far East were obliged to pass through the North Atlantic on their way to and from these destinations. Finally, it was within easy striking-distance of the North Sea and English Channel. From time to time, disputes with European countries led to the Straits of Gibraltar being closed against ships from Algiers or Tripoli, but this made no difference to corsairs or pirates sailing from Salé. Their port was on Morocco's Atlantic coast and so they had a free run of both the Atlantic and also the seas surrounding Western Europe.

It was not always easy for the countries being harassed by Barbary corsairs to tell from where the ships originated and often they were simply referred to as 'Turkish' or 'Barbary'. Sometimes though, it was possible to be more precise in the identification and when this was possible during the mid-seventeenth century, it seemed that ships from Salé were very active off the coasts of Britain and Spain. Records show that on 20 September 1635, to give one example, 'six Sali men-of-war' boarded a ship off the coast of Cornwall and took the crew to sell into slavery (Eliot, 1881).

The ruler in Rabat, which was only separated from Salé by the Bou Regreg river, must, at least to begin with, have thought that allowing the refugees from Spain to settle in a neglected part of his country was a sharp move. After all, the newcomers were no trouble at all to him and he received 10 per cent of all their plunder from the attacks on European shipping. He was to benefit from their operations without having to do anything at all.

One of the curiosities about the Barbary corsairs is the frequency with which European exiles from their own countries, men who had supposedly converted to Islam, became either the captains of ship or the leaders of entire fleets of corsairs. This is exactly what happened in Salé a few years after the settlement began. A short while after the arrival of the Moriscos, a Dutchman called Jan Janszoon, who had himself been captured by a Barbary ship and then converted to Islam and taken the name of Murat Reis, settled in Salé. He had his own ship and after one or two forays, he decided that there was little point in continuing to give a tenth of the proceeds of their activities to the Sultan. Why not keep it all for themselves? So it was that under the leadership of Janszoon, Salé was declared an independent republic, owing no allegiance to the sultan. After a brief and unsuccessful siege, the sultan was forced to accept this situation, at least for the time being, and so began the world's first pirate republic.

Jan Janszoon van Harlem must have been an extraordinary man, as even the briefest study of his life shows. He was born in Harlem in 1575 and as far as we known the only calling he ever pursued was that of seagoing privateer or corsair. He was born during the Eighty Years War, a conflict which lasted for the whole of his life. The territories which today comprise the Netherlands, Belgium and Luxembourg were at one time provinces of the Hapsburg monarchy, ruled by Philip II of Spain. The Eighty Years War was their long struggle to break free of this domination. In 1581 some of these provinces managed to drive out the Spanish and establish the Dutch Republic. At the age of 25 Jan Janszoon obtained letters of marque and began sailing as a privateer on behalf of the Republic.

The Dutch Republic's enemy was of course Spain, whose armies still occupied a large part of the Netherlands, and they were happy for men like Janszoon to attack Spanish shipping for their own profit. If it was expedient, privateers could be disowned and their activities described as piracy, even by those who had commissioned them. This might be necessary, for instance, if another country regarded an attack by a privateer as a *casus belli*. The English played this game as well, of course, being happy to see men like Francis Drake play havoc with Spanish shipping, as long as it did not precipitate a formal state of war with other nations. Of course, the thin line between privateering and piracy was easily crossed. England's Walter Raleigh was another well-known privateer, but when he went too far and his exploits precipitated the threat of war with Spain, King James was happy to see him executed.

From the beginning of his career, Jan Janszoon sailed exceedingly close to the wind. At times, he would raise the flag of the Dutch Republic and at others the red crescent of the Ottomans. Which flag he sailed under was purely a matter of expedience and depended upon how much treasure he was likely to gain. Of course, he was working a field which was already crowded with competitors, some of whom were stronger and better armed than he. He had a very good run for his money though, lasting for almost 20 years as part-time Dutch privateer and sometimes freelance pirate. In 1618 though, he was captured near Lanzarote by some genuine Barbary corsairs and taken back to Algiers as a slave. It was a temporary reverse though, because he decided to 'turn Turk' or convert to Islam. To what extent this decision was motivated by religious fervour and how much it was simply a practical means to improve his lot, we are never likely at this late stage to discover.

It did not take Jan Janszoon, or Murat Reis as he was now styling himself, to gain his freedom and escape from Algiers. His new master was keen to have such an experienced sailor on his ship and when in the course of a skirmish the real captain of the ship upon which he was now serving was killed, Janszoon seized control and set off for Morocco. He did not intend any longer to remain a simple privateer.

The 15,000 or so Spanish Muslims who had settled in Salé were, as Janszoon saw it, in sore need of a determined leader and he had a good idea of who would be ideally suited to provide the necessary leadership. In 1619, just a year after his fortunes had reached their lowest ebb and he had been a helpless slave, this wandering and rootless Dutchman had somehow persuaded the Spanish settlers to appoint him not only as their Grand Admiral, but also president of the new republic. True, he had to rule by means of a council of a dozen other corsairs, but everybody in Salé knew who was really the boss.

Only unusual times could allow an adventurer like Jan Janszoon to take charge of his very own state. There were two separate and distinct civil wars in the offing in that part of the world and the threat of chaos inclined many people to seek a strong leader and Janszoon was certainly that. In Morocco as a whole, the sultan, Zaydan An-Nasser, was struggling to maintain control, his authority being challenged not only by various restive tribes, but also a rival dynasty who felt that they had a strong claim to the throne. Not only that, but the Spanish king had long had his eyes on Morocco and was waiting for a chance to land his own troops there and carve off a piece of the kingdom as his own. It was for these reasons that the men of Salé had felt confident enough to set at naught the sultan's authority and proclaim their independence. The sultan had enough problems already, without being compelled to fight a war on his own doorstep.

Once the sultan had shown that he was unable to assault Salé by force of arms and until some greater power arose in Morocco, Janszoon and those running the new republic with him were reasonably safe from any outside threat; at least for the time being. There was another struggle being waged though, one which in the end caused Jan Janszoon to leave his cosy little domain and strike out once more into the outside world. For the next decade or so though, he was secure enough.

While they had been contributing a share of their loot with the leader of a state, it was possible, at a stretch, to call the eighteen ships operating out of Salé privateers. With this fig leaf of respectability removed, Janszoon and his cronies were revealed for what they really were. He might well have taken to calling himself a Grand Admiral, but the little statelet which he and a dozen others now ruled had no other source of income than the ships, men and treasure which they could steal at sea. A constitution of sorts was drawn up, with provision for the election each year of a council to run the new republic and, recognizing the reality of the situation, the sultan appointed Jan Janszoon governor of Salé. This was an attempt to pretend that he still had any kind of say over what went on in the new city which was so close to Rabat that it could be seen across the estuary of the Bou Regreg.

Being outside the Mediterranean, Salé and the surrounding territory were not impinging upon the Ottoman's ambitions and so they could afford to ignore the Turks. Spain was a menace but was still occupied with the Eighty Years War. It was a wonderful time to be a corsair and the ships sailing from Salé had a free run at any shipping which passed along the coast. They took spices and gold being brought back to Europe from the east, commandeered the ships for their own and sold the crews on to slavers from one or other of the Ottoman provinces. The corsairs from the city became known as the Salé Rovers and they were feared by everybody. It was little wonder that Daniel Defoe worked them into his most famous book, for that gave it a pleasingly topical touch.

All good things come to an end and it was clear to Jan Janszoon after a few years that things were not going to remain so happily in his favour in the city which he had chosen to make his home forever. He and those running the place were members of an elite, the first Spaniards to arrive in Salé having been better off than the motley crowd who later turned up after the Edicts of Expulsion came into force. The later settlers began to be dissatisfied about being treated like peasants and tensions grew, until the situation became violent. This was all in the future though and for a time, life went very smoothly for the Salé Rovers. Apart from the lucrative business in selling the goods stolen from merchant ships, there was money to be made from charging fees for ships of other nations to dock in the harbour and take on provisions. For those about to embark on a long voyage around the Cape of Good Hope, Salé was a handy port to call at for supplies.

By 1627, the simmering tensions between the different groups of Spanish settlers who had founded Salé were threatening to erupt into open confrontation. Janszoon felt that it was time for him to move on and he simply loaded up a ship and abandoned the city of which he was still theoretically the Grand Admiral. He relocated to Algiers and, being nominally a Muslim, was able to continue his career of piracy as a privateer, operating on behalf of the Ottomans. At one point, he occupied the Isle of Lundy, off the coast of Devon, and it was he who led both the raid on the Irish village of Baltimore and also the expedition to Iceland, both of which we looked at in a previous chapter.

The strange republic of Salé managed to continue for another 40 years after Jan Janszoon's departure. There were ups and downs before it was finally retaken by the Moroccans. In 1629, for example, France became very irate about attacks on their ships and sent Admiral Isaac de Razilly with a fleet composed of seven ships, namely the *Licorne, Saint-Louis, Griffon, Catherine, Hambourg, Sainte-Anne* and *Saint-Jean*. On 20 July, the town was bombarded by the admiral, leading the corsairs to give a wide berth to French ships, at least for a time. The beginning of the end for this unique experiment in statehood came in 1631, when the Alaouite dynasty ousted the Saadis who had been ruling an increasingly fragmented kingdom. It is the Aloaouites who still rule Morocco to this day.

Even after Salé had been brought back into the fold and reincorporated into Morocco, the corsairs still operated from Moroccan territory, the sultan once again taking a share of the plunder. It was this policy of allowing ships from Rabat and other ports to cruise the Atlantic looking for slaves and other profitable goods which led to one of the most extraordinary episodes in the history of the country, which took place when a Scottish woman became empress of Morocco.

A hundred years after the end of the Republic of Salé, the corsairs of Morocco were still roaming the North Atlantic seeking prey and in 1769 came upon a ship bound for America, which was full of men and women emigrating from Scotland. Among them was an attractive redheaded and green-eyed teenager who was escaping from an unhappy family life. Helen Gloag was 19 in May 1769, when she took ship for South Carolina, a popular part of America for those from Scotland (Bruce, 1998). It had a ready-made community of Scottish settlers and so the blacksmith's daughter expected to be able to fit in without too much difficulty. Two weeks after they left British waters, a small fleet of corsairs moved in and captured the British ship. It was the women who were chiefly wanted and when she reached Morocco, Helen Gloag found herself being sold to a wealthy Moroccan merchant. This man, seeking to ingratiate himself with his sovereign, Mohammed ben Abdallah of Morocco, made a gift of her to the sultan.

Mohammed ben Abdallah was something of a reformer and had been curtailing the exploits of the corsairs in his own country, at least to some extent, but he found himself entranced by the beauty of the woman who had been presented to him and added her to his harem. It seems that the sultan or emperor of Morocco actually fell in love with this strange beauty and, not content with keeping her as one of his concubines, he elevated her to the position of wife. He already had three wives, but it soon began to be thought that his latest wife was his favourite. At least, she was granted considerably more freedom than was usual in such circumstances, which was interpreted as a mark of her special status to the sultan.

For 20 years Helen Gloag's life was like something from a romantic novel. Beginning as a blacksmith's daughter, she became in swift succession slave, member of the harem, sultan's wife and then empress. She was allowed to write letters abroad and maintained correspondence with her family in Scotland. Her brother Robert came to visit her. After bearing two children, both boys, and because of her special position, it was assumed that one of her sons would become sultan upon his father's death. It was not to be. When Mohammed ben Abdallah died in 1790, another of his sons quickly made a play for power and seized the throne. As a way of disposing with dangerous rivals for the kingdom, he ordered that Helen Gloag's boys should both be murdered.

Scope for the corsairs in the Atlantic Ocean was much reduced towards the end of the eighteenth century, due to the war fought between France and Britain. The Atlantic Ocean, North Sea and English Channel were increasingly full of French and British warships and both navies had a short way with those whom they regarded as pirates. The Barbary corsairs were still flourishing in the Mediterranean, but Morocco's days as a leader in the field were over.

Before his death Mohammed ben Abdallah signed a treaty with the United States, entering into negotiations with this end in mind before America had even stopped fighting its war of independence from Britain. There was some delay in arranging the thing though and the sultan adopted a most singular and striking way of speeding up the process.

Sultan Mohammed ben Abdallah wished to see his country adopting some Western habits. In particular, he was keen to reduce the size of his standing army. Under the traditional system in Morocco, the army played a vital role in collecting taxes. Without the threat of armed force, it would have been very hard to extract any revenue from some of the wilder parts of the kingdom. The sultan thought that trade with other countries might not only be beneficial to his economy but could also bring enough money that he would not need to send troops to tax his people. As part of this strategy, he was determined to open up his country's ports to ships from America and Europe. It was to prove more difficult than Mohammed ben Abdallah expected.

There was another and even more pressing reason for the Moroccans to begin trading with the world and that was that there was a shortage of food which, in another few years, was likely to turn into famine. There was an urgent need to start importing wheat into the country and this meant opening up the ports to foreign shipping. With this in mind, on 20 December 1777, while America was still trying to break free of Britain, the sultan issued a proclamation in which he specified a number of nations which were welcome to use any and all of Morocco's ports. These were America, Russia, Malta, Sardinia, Prussia, Naples, Hungary, Leghorn, Genoa, and Germany. Whether because they had more important matters to concern themselves with at that time, other than establishing international commerce, or for some other reason, there was no response to this message from America. After re-issuing his wish for friendship with the new republic, Mohammed ben Abdallah had to wait until December 1780 until he received the following message from America;

> We the Congress of the 13 United States of North America, have been informed of your Majesty's favorable regard to the interests of the people we represent, which has been communicated by Monsieur Etienne d'Audibert Caille of Sale, Consul of Foreign nations unrepresented in your Majesty's states. We assure you of our earnest desire to cultivate a sincere and firm peace and friendship with your Majesty and to make it lasting to all posterity. Should any of the subjects of our states come within the ports of your Majesty's territories, we flatter ourselves they will receive the benefit of your protection and benevolence. You may assure yourself of every protection and assistance to your subjects from the people of these states

whenever and wherever they may have it in their power. We pray your Majesty may enjoy long life and uninterrupted prosperity.

Despite this promising start, negotiations with America dragged on for years and in the end the sultan struck upon what he saw as good way of speeding up the diplomatic process. He had offered the carrot of safety and free trade; perhaps it was now time for the stick? The *Betsy* was a 300-ton brig sailing across the Atlantic towards the Straits of Gibraltar and on 11 October 1784 it was boarded by Moroccan corsairs in the time-honoured pirate style, men with cutlasses held in the teeth and pistols tucked in their belts leaping onto the deck of the American merchant vessel (Parker, 2004). The crew of eleven was then taken ashore and held in Morocco. This certainly had the effect of making diplomacy move more quickly, because in next to no time at all the American Congress had authorized a payment of $80,000 to be made to Morocco, as part of a peace treaty with that country. The Moroccan–American Treaty of Friendship which was subsequently signed has never been violated. Morocco was the first country in the world to recognize the newly independent republic of America and for almost 250 years the two nations have enjoyed amicable relations.

New countries often find that they are not included in the arrangements which older nations have formed over the years. It is customary to treat newcomers on the international stage with a certain degree of caution, at least until it is certain that they will last. This happened of course with the newly-formed British republic under Oliver Cromwell and it is what happened with America at the end of the eighteenth century. The civilized world consisted essentially at that time of Europe and their monarchies. The very notion of republics was felt to be more than a little subversive and there was no great enthusiasm for seeing a successful instance of this model becoming accepted. It might, after all give the citizens of older and more settled countries ideas. If America could get by without a king, queen or emperor, then why shouldn't the same system work in Britain? It was an alarming thought.

The British in particular had no wish to see a former colony flourish after breaking free of their rule. It would provide a very disturbing precedent for other colonies who might be less than enchanted with British rule. The British government of the day did everything possible therefore both to keep America closely bound by trade and also to discourage other nations from recognizing America or forming commercial relationships with the country. With all the disruption in the North Sea and English Channel caused by the war between Britain and France, it was fairly easy to discourage American shipping from dealing directly with Western Europe. The Mediterranean though was another matter and there was, in theory, little that could be done to prevent American merchant ships sailing through the Straits of Gibraltar and then striking deals with Italy, France or the Ottoman Empire. There was a way to make life difficult for such vessels, however, and the British ruthlessly exploited this. They had themselves long ago come to an accommodation with the provinces of the Barbary Coast, whereby they paid regular sums of money for their shipping to be left in peace. This protection had been extended to American ships, as long as America was a British colony. Now, the case was altered.

In the next chapter we shall be looking at how America became a world power and the fascinating fact that it was the Barbary corsairs who were largely responsible for the adoption of this role.

Chapter 10

America Enters the World Stage

O ne aspect of the trade in white slaves which has entirely been forgotten is its role in causing America to become an international power and view itself as the proper authority to enforce order in the world. This tendency on the part of the United States to act as the world's policeman is exceedingly marked today and has its origins in the slave trade of the Barbary Coast. The means by which American power is projected around the world is usually their navy. Just as Britain did at the height of the empire, gunboats are sent to restive areas, accompanied by submarines and aircraft carriers. The United States Navy was itself founded as a direct response to the actions of the various North African rulers at which we have so far been looking in this book.

By the closing decades of the eighteenth century, Britain and one or two other countries had reached a *modus vivendi* with the semi-autonomous Ottoman provinces of the Barbary Coast, one which suited all sides. By paying annual 'tribute' to the rulers of places such as Algiers and Tripoli, the British were assured that their vessels would be left alone. This was cheaper than launching wars in the Mediterranean and also more advantageous from a purely mercantile point of view. With the British ships free to sail the Mediterranean, the corsairs would be forced to turn their attentions to other merchant ships, those belonging to commercial rivals of the British. This would have the effect of making Britain the dominant trading power in the region. What was being operated by the various territories of North Africa was, in effect, a protection racket which happened to suit British interests.

The problem with paying ransom in this way is of course that it only encourages others to try the same tactic, seeing your country as a soft touch. This happened to Germany in the late twentieth century, when a situation arose which was very similar to that of the tribute being paid in the early nineteenth century to the Barbary States. We will look at this in the next chapter. One cannot help, when thinking about the whole idea of paying tribute to avoid unpleasantness, but to be reminded again of paying the Dane-Geld. Rudyard Kipling summed up the case succinctly in his poem *Dane-Geld* (Kipling, 1911). Part of this poem reads;

> And that is called paying the Dane-Geld;
> But we've proved it again and again,
> That if once you have paid him the Dane-Geld
> You never get rid of the Dane.

The closing lines of the poem set out what was eventually to become the official American policy as regards paying tribute and ransom to the states of the Barbary Coast;

> So when you are requested to pay up or be molested,
> You will find it better policy to say: —
> 'We never pay *any*-one Dane-Geld,
> No matter how trifling the cost;
> For the end of that game is oppression and shame,
> And the nation that plays it is lost!'

There were several false starts and America certainly began paying the Dane-Geld, but then realized that it was a mistake and adopted a firmer position, one which signalled the slow but inexorable rise of the United States as it became a world power.

Britain and the rest of Europe had been struggling to deal with the problem represented by the corsairs sailing from North Africa for over 200 years. It was, after all, their problem; countries such as France, Spain and Italy were separated from the ports from which the slavers and pirates sailed by a few hundred miles of water at most. This makes it very surprising that it should have been the newly-established republic of America which took the lead in putting an end once and for all to the nuisance. It was particularly surprising that the new country should have launched such an initiative so soon after being founded. The American War of Independence ended in 1781 and within a mere 20 years of the last engagement of that war at the Battle of Yorktown, the fledging nation had formed its own navy and was fighting a fierce war in the Mediterranean.

We saw in the last chapter how European countries had come to accommodations with the Ottoman territories and independent states of North Africa and found it convenient to pay, rather than run the risk of their merchant vessels being boarded and the crew abducted. Wars are expensive and from a strictly mercantile point of view, it was without doubt cheaper just to send regular 'tribute' to a country, rather than be obliged to mount naval attacks upon their territory. It was an arrangement which seemed to suit all parties well enough and might have continued indefinitely had the revolution in America not upset the proverbial applecart.

British ships were not molested as they passed through the Mediterranean, partly because of the money which was being paid by their government to the rulers of the various nations, but also due to the fact that any attempt to interfere with British shipping would bring down retribution in the form of a naval bombardment. Once America had beaten the British though and was no longer a colony, their merchant ships were denied this protection. Indeed, the British quickly informed the nations of North Africa explicitly that they could, if they wished, prey upon American ships and as far as Britain was concerned, good luck to them! Some might think this more than a little vindictive on the part of the British, but they were, after all, smarting from the loss of one of their largest colonies.

Perhaps a word or two of explanation might be necessary here to explain why the corsairs of the Barbary Coast had begun attacking ships again after the resounding defeat which they suffered at the hands of Spain in 1784. We read of this in Chapter 8 and it certainly looked at that time as though the days of the corsairs in the Mediterranean were at an end. So they might have been if Europe had not once again started to tear itself apart in a series of wars which were so widespread across such a large part of the globe that some historians regard them as having constituted the first real world war.

The French Revolution began in 1789 and from the beginning, other European countries were uneasy at seeing a monarch deposed by the ordinary people. This particular monarch's wife happened to be the sister of Leopold II, the Holy Roman Emperor, and he rallied support against the revolutionary regime, with a number of countries determined to come to the French king's aid. Throughout the 1790s France fought against Austria and Prussia and then Portugal and Spain. In 1798, the war spread to the Middle East, with a French invasion of Egypt. The French Revolutionary Wars segued seamlessly into the Napoleonic Wars, once Napoleon Bonaparte had seized control of France, and continued until 1815. For over 20 years, war raged from the Middle East to Scandinavia, from the West Indies to Moscow and from the North Sea to South Africa.

With the nations of Europe fighting each other in much the way that they had during the Eighty Years War and the Thirty Years War, it was the perfect time for the corsairs of the Barbary Coast to begin their slave raids and seizure of merchant ships once more. It was unlikely that any European country would be able to spare the naval resources to attack Algiers or Tripoli while they were struggling with their neighbours. They reckoned though without a country which was probably unknown at that time to many people on the Barbary Coast.

It is beyond the scope of this book to delve deeply into the history of the American War of Independence, but the aftermath of this conflict has considerable bearing on the ending of the Barbary pirates and corsairs and their enslavement of Europeans and so at least the background must be sketched. Britain had a very healthy economic link with the American colonies in the 1770s, one which was very beneficial to Britain. America, together with Britain's Caribbean colonies, were very useful, not only as a source for imported goods such as sugar and tobacco, but also as a market for the export of goods manufactured in

Britain. It was for this reason that the loss of America was so galling to Britain.

We have all heard the expression, 'No taxation without representation', which became popular just before the war between Britain and America broke out. As an imperial power, Britain regarded the colonies essentially as a means to enrich herself and trade was conducted with them on terms which were most advantageous to Britain. This, of course, led to the so-called 'Boston Tea Party' in 1773, when tea being imported to America from India was thrown into the sea at Boston's harbour. The American point of view was that the thirteen colonies which at that time made up America should not have taxes imposed upon them unless they had representatives in the British parliament who could stand up for the American point of view.

The war which broke out in 1775 lasted in theory until 1783, although the fighting ended two years earlier. It was all a great shock to the British and they did all that they could to make life difficult for the breakaway colonies. It was essential for the fledgling nation's survival that America was free to trade as it wished with the rest of the world, but the British, in a spirit of vindictiveness, chose to try and sabotage American international commerce. In 1783, the year that the war between Britain and America formally ended, a book was published in England with the longwinded title *Observations on the commerce of the American states with Europe and the West Indies: including the several articles of import and export, and on the tendency of a bill now depending in Parliament*. It was written by the Earl of Sheffield and contained a number of mischievous assertions and suggestions which showed how the minds of some people in Britain were working. For example, the author wrote that, 'The Americans cannot protect themselves as they cannot pretend to have a Navy' (Holroyd, 1783).

There was more than mere spite in the British attitude to the idea of America trading openly with Europe. Like all mercantile powers, Britain's aim in commerce was to hold a monopoly, or the nearest thing to that state of affairs which could be achieved. The last thing they wanted under those circumstances was to see another country, especially one selling goods such as tobacco, for which there was a great demand in eighteenth-century Europe, entering the market. Having Algiers and other Barbary States harassing American ships and making life difficult for them suited the British so well that, strange as it might seem, Algiers became seen as an ally of Britain. Benjamin Franklin, who in 1783 was the American ambassador to France, wrote in July of that year about the situation as he understood it. After discussing the possibility of importing manufactured goods from Hungary, via the port of Trieste in the Mediterranean, he wrote of the corsairs;

> I think it not improbable that those rovers may be privately encouraged by the English to fall upon us, and to prevent our interference in the carrying trade; for I have in London heard it is a maxim among the merchants that if *there were no Algiers it would be worth England's while to build one*. (Wharton, 1888)

It was perfectly true, as the Earl of Sheffield wrote, that the new country of America had no navy to begin with. There were a few coastal vessels, to guard harbours and mount patrols, but there was no need for any ocean-going warships. During the war with Britain, they had had a modest fleet suitable for minor skirmishes in what they saw as their territorial waters, but nothing intended to travel further than a few miles from shore. After the British had been beaten, thoughts were turned more towards consolidation and the building-up of the nation, rather than military matters. This economic development would be accomplished by, among other means, trading with the rest of the world. This meant at that time, essentially, trading with Europe. It was in Europe that goods were being manufactured and if America wished to become a modern, industrialized power, then they would need to import machinery and all manner of other things from Europe which could not be obtained anywhere else in the world, while at the same time selling their own produce.

The first intimation for America that they might need to consider starting a navy came the year after the end of the War of Independence, when an American ship was seized in the North Atlantic by a corsair based in Morocco. A month earlier Thomas Jefferson, one of the founding fathers of the American Revolution, had already been considering how shipping could be protected from the depredations of the North African provinces of the Ottoman Empire. On 11 November 1784, he wrote to James Monroe asking, 'Would it not be better to offer them an equal treaty. If they refuse, why not go to war with them?'. After the merchant ship was captured, he wrote again to Monroe, setting out what was, eventually, to become the accepted view in America; that it would be better to adopt a firm line of attacks from what we would today perhaps call 'rogue states';

> Our trade to Portugal, Spain, and the Mediterranean is annihilated unless we do something decisive. Tribute or war is the usual alternative of these pirates. If we yield the former, it will require sums which our people will feel. Why not begin a navy then and decide on war? We cannot begin in a better cause nor against a weaker foe.

Jefferson has seen, quite correctly, that it would be better policy to offer war as an alternative to paying tribute. Unfortunately, Jefferson's was a minority view and paying out $80,000 to Morocco seemed at the time a shrewd investment to protect American shipping passing across the North Atlantic and entering the Mediterranean. The Moroccans had for years been trying to secure a treaty with America and hijacking one of their ships had really just been a gambit to speed up the negotiations a little. We remember however what Kipling wrote about paying the Dane-Geld; 'That if once you have paid him the Dane-Geld, You never get rid of the Dane'. So it proved in this case, because just as the Americans were congratulating themselves on their diplomacy and ability to handle foreign affairs as skilfully as any of the older European nations, two more of their ships were seized by corsairs. Once America had agreed to pay ransom to one country, all the others felt that they deserved no less.

On 25 July 1785 corsairs from Algiers boarded and captured the American schooner *Maria*. A week later, the *Dauphin* was also taken and both ships were taken to Algiers and their crews were enslaved. These actions were accompanied by a declaration of war on the United States by Dey Mohammed, who was the ruler of Algiers. Being so generous towards Morocco had not purchased safety, but only given other ruthless men the idea that targeting America ships might be a profitable venture.

The new nation was clearly viewed as militarily weak and in no position to do otherwise than surrender to any demands made upon it. When Britain had made deals with the Barbary nations and agreed to pay tribute, they had negotiated from a position of strength, in that nobody was under any illusion that if pushed too hard, the Royal Navy would sail into the Mediterranean and begin bombarding the ports on the North African coast. The Americans patently had no such capability; they did not even have a navy. Little wonder then that everybody felt able to shove them around and seize their ships at will. Since they had no bargaining power at all, all that the United States could do was to plead for lenient terms in any treaty and agreement to pay tribute. The Dey of Algiers must have been delighted with himself and to increase pressure on America, he authorized his men to take more American ships and bring their crew-members to be sold in the slave markets.

The humiliating situation in which the Americans found themselves could be ultimately resolved only by the country transforming itself into a serious naval power; a process which could not of course happen overnight. Quite apart from the logistics of building warships, equipping them and raising a force of men able to operate such vessels, a political leader would need to take command; a man unafraid of fighting a war, should it prove necessary.

Although it is not really germane to the subject of white slavery and the Barbary corsairs, it might be mentioned that the United States was being pressured by the privateers of another country at this time; namely the French Republic. The French felt that as a fellow, newly-formed republic, America might wish to join an alliance with them in their wars against Britain. This was not at all the wish of America, which simply wished to be left alone to trade peacefully, without entering any foreign wars. Angered by this refusal, the government of France changed tack and suddenly demanded tribute themselves from the United States, in the form of a payment of $50,000 and a loan of $10,000,000.

It was to be over a decade before Algiers and the United States signed a treaty which was intended to protect American shipping from being molested in the future. By that time, corsairs from Algiers had taken another eleven American ships, with the aim of piling pressure on America to come to some accommodation with them. The treaty, when it was signed, made provision for America to pay the astounding sum of $642,000, with an annual tribute of $21,000 to be paid in the future. Not only that, but four warships were to be given to Algiers, including a 36-gun frigate. In return, the 131 sailors who had been taken prisoner and made slaves were to be freed.

It is possible to gauge just how hard were the conditions under which slaves lived and worked at this time when we learn that of the 131 healthy and active men who had been taken between 1785 and 1796, no fewer than a third had died. Just eighty-five men remained alive and were able to return to their homes (Elleman, Rosenberg & Forbes, 2010). Nothing could more clearly illustrate how arduous was the life of a slave in North Africa at this time.

It was obviously by this time to everybody that simply paying all the demands for tribute would not put an end to the problems which America was experiencing in trying to trade peacefully in the countries around the Mediterranean. No sooner had the treaty with Algiers been signed, than the other Barbary States began asking why they too should not be entitled to the same terms, if they refrained from preying upon American ships.

John Adams and Thomas Jefferson, both future presidents of the United States, being respectively the second and third men to hold that office, had exchanged letters about the problem of the dealing with the Barbary States, and the virtues of the two possible means of tackling the threat posed by the corsairs, as early as 1786. Both men were agreed that the question was one of *realpolitik*, rather than any sound, ethical principle. They knew that money would have to be expended to allow American commerce with Europe to continue unhindered, the only question being whether it was cheaper to hand over regular and relatively modest sums as tribute, as opposed to investing a very large sum in building and training a permanent navy. Adams, who was president between 1797 and 1801, favoured the option of paying tribute, however distasteful he found it, on purely economic grounds. On 3 July 1786, Adams wrote to Thomas Jefferson, saying of the Barbary States;

> 1. We may at this Time, have a Peace with them, in Spight of all the Intrigues of the English or others to prevent it, for a Sum of Money.

> 2. We never Shall have Peace, though France, Spain, England and Holland Should use all their Influence in our favour without a Sum of Money.

> 3. That neither the Benevolence of France nor the Malevolence of England will be ever able materially to diminish or Increase the Sum.

> 4. The longer the Negotiation is delayed, the larger will be the Demand.

> From these Premisses I conclude it to be wisest for Us to negotiate and pay the necessary Sum, without Loss of Time.

In retrospect, we may see that such a policy was a recipe for disaster, because of course human greed knows no bounds, but at the time it seemed reasonable enough, although Thomas Jefferson was not persuaded. That Jefferson and not Adams had the clearest understanding of the matter may be seen when we look at the subsequent developments after America had signed their treaty with Algiers.

Because other Barbary States were demanding tribute and threatening to attack American ships following the signing of the treaty with Algiers, it was thought expedient to sign similar treaties with Tunis and Tripoli. These cost America $160,000, in addition to various goods and personal presents for the rulers of the territories. Such gifts added considerably to the expense of the tribute. The Pasha of Tunis, for instance, received a pair of pistols which were covered in gold and set with diamonds.

George Washington was president until 1797 and gave his reluctant approval to the increasingly large sums of money being handed over to North Africa as the price for trading in the Mediterranean. By the time that John Adams became the second American president in 1797, it was fairly obvious that the whole thing had got out of hand. By now, the government had handed over $1.25 million to Morocco, Algiers, Tunis and Tripoli (Fremont-Barnes, 2006). Considering that the entire annual budget of the United States amounted only to $6 million or so, it is easy to see that this was not a situation which could continue indefinitely.

During Adams' presidency, America began to fall behind with the payment of tribute, causing threats to be issued that the taking of American ships and their crews might be resumed. William Eaton, who was the American consul in Tunis, had a better understanding of the state of affairs than his political masters in Washington. He wrote that;

> there is no access to the permanent friendship of these states without paving the way with gold or cannonballs; and the proper question is which method is preferable.

In the next chapter, we shall encounter William Eaton again and see that he himself favoured the use of cannonballs, rather than the payment of gold. The problem was that despite the signing of carefully-worded treaties, the individuals in charge of places such as Tunis and Tripoli were greedy and envious. If they thought that the Americans were giving money to another state, then they wanted the same, regardless of any agreement which was in place. The treaty signed between the United States and Tripoli in 1796 was a case in point. It provided for 'firm and perpetual peace and friendship' between the two nations and Article 10 included the words that 'no periodical tribute or further payment is ever to be made by either party'. Instead, a one-off payment of 40,000 Spanish dollars was made, along with a quantity of jewellery. The only provision for any future gifts was in an addendum to the treaty, in which America agreed that each time a new consul was appointed, he would bring with him the sum of 12,000 Spanish dollars, as well as considerable amounts of timber.

Notwithstanding the provisions of the agreement which had been signed, the ruler of Tripoli began to express his dissatisfaction as the years passed, claiming that other Barbary States were receiving more gifts than he himself. In 1799 and 1800, his complaints increased in frequency and he made the explicit threat that if something were not done, he would tear up the treaty and declare war on the United States. He had chosen an inauspicious time to try and bully the Americans, because an election was being held at the end of 1800, to decide if John Adams would remain in office or if he would be replaced with Thomas Jefferson. The Bashaw or Pasha of Tripoli knew nothing of the democratic process and in February 1801, he repudiated the 'firm and perpetual' treaty of friendship.

Chapter 11

The Barbary Wars

O n 10 May 1801 the Bashaw of Tripoli officially declared war on the United States. Four days later he ordered the flagpole outside the house used by the American ambassador to be cut down, a symbolic act of great significance. It was intended to signal the beginning of active hostilities between the two nations. Had he but known it, the Bashaw could scarcely have chosen a worse or less auspicious time to confront America. He had been so much accustomed to demanding, and receiving, vast sums of money from other countries in return for not attacking their ships and enslaving their crews, that perhaps he hardly gave the matter more than a moment's cursory thought. He had lately declared war on Sweden and was holding a number of that country's citizens. Sweden swiftly capitulated and sent a huge ransom in order to obtain their freedom.

When the Bashaw announced the start of a war between his own country and the United States, Thomas Jefferson, one of the founding fathers of the republic, had for 15 years been expressing doubts about the wisdom of paying 'tribute' to the Barbary States in an effort to prevent them from attacking America's merchant vessels. He had correctly foreseen that such a course of action would not provide a permanent solution to the problem of the corsair attacks and that sooner or later it would be necessary to adopt a firmer line. Writing as early as 1784, Jefferson had expressed his views as follows;

> The question is whether their peace or war will be cheapest? But is it a question which should be addressed to our Honor as well as our Avarice? Nor does it respect us as to these pyrates only, but as to the nations of Europe. If we wish our commerce to be free and uninsulted, we must let these nations see that

we have an energy which at present they disbelieve. The low opinion they entertain of our powers cannot fail to involve us soon in a naval war. (Boyd, Bryan & Hutter, 1953)

Jefferson's point was that even if it proved cheaper to pay tribute than to resort to military action, this would, in the long run, be a false economy. If America were thought to be too weak to defend its interests by war, then not only the Barbary States but the countries of Europe too would regard the country with contempt and feel that they could take any advantage with impunity. He saw the disputes with Algiers, Tunis and Tripoli as an opportunity to show the world that the United States was not a country to be trifled with.

It was now that Thomas Jefferson used a phrase which has become very well-known and in the minds of many people associated with him. In fact, when he declared firmly, 'Millions for defence, but not one cent for tribute', he was using a variation of the words of America's former ambassador to France at the time that the French were demanding tribute of their own from the fledgling American republic. Charles C. Pinckney said, when France was trying to extort money on the threat of unleashing their navy and privateers against American ships, 'Not a penny – not a sixpence!' Shortly after saying this, a congressman enlarged Pinckney's words to the familiar, 'Millions for defence, but not a cent for tribute!' Since it summed up succinctly the new president's view of the matter when dealing with the regimes of North Africa, it was only natural that he should repeat the phrase himself.

It is to be doubted if the Bashaw of Tripoli had even heard of Jefferson before he launched a war against America, let alone that he was aware of the new president's views and opinions on the situation in the Mediterranean. It was a fatal miscalculation, because when Thomas Jefferson was inaugurated as the third president of the United States on 4 March 1801, he was almost immediately presented with the opportunity to put into practice the policies which he had been advocating for the last decade and a half. Some indication of his determination may be seen when we learn that even before learning of

Tripoli's declaration of war, the new president had ordered two-thirds of the newly-formed United States Navy to sail for the Mediterranean.

Two-thirds of the United States Navy sounds a not inconsiderable naval force, a veritable armada, perhaps. In fact, America at that time had a mere six ships, four of which were despatched to deal with Tripoli. Although news travelled slowly at that time and it would be another month or so before Washington knew for sure that the Bashaw had actually declared war against them, Thomas Jefferson knew which way the wind was blowing. At a Cabinet meeting on 15 May, it was unanimously agreed to send a task force to protect American shipping and deal promptly with anybody who was minded to interfere with any ships flying the American flag. On 1 June 1801 four ships, three frigates and a schooner, left the harbour at Hampton Roads, which lay between Virginia and North Carolina. Captain Richard Dale was in charge of the expedition and had been granted the honorary rank of 'Commodore', because he was in command of more than one ship. His orders were very clear and specific. If, when once he had crossed the Atlantic and arrived at Gibraltar, he learned that war had been declared, he was to arrange his forces;

> so as best to protect our commerce & chastise their insolence—
> by sinking, burning or destroying their ships & Vessels
> wherever you shall find them. (Swanson, 1939)

Dale was further ordered that in the event that he found himself at war, he was not to approach the Bashaw to initiate any negotiations, but to fight on until he was himself asked for a ceasefire.

The appearance of four heavily-armed American ships off the North African coast created something of a stir and when they arrived at Tripoli on 24 July, there was great anxiety among the inhabitants, from the ordinary sailors all the way up to the Bashaw himself. It was apparent that the rules had suddenly and unexpectedly changed.

Keen though the new president was to assert his country's power, he had no intention of fighting all the Barbary States simultaneously and in addition to his instructions to be ruthless if he encountered and aggression from Tripoli, Commodore Dale also carried the overdue tribute which was owed under previous treaties to Algiers and Tunis. Those countries must, however, have realized that the days of their being able to run what amounted in effect to an international protection racket were drawing to a close (Lambert, 2007).

To anybody other than historians, the USS *Enterprise* will be forever associated with the television science fiction series *Star Trek*. There is however a reason that the fictional starship was so named and it is because there had previously been famous American ships of that name, one of which was a schooner which sailed as part of the squadron of ships sent to the Mediterranean in the summer of 1801. That USS *Enterprise* had been launched in 1799 and was commanded by Lieutenant Andrew Sterett. She was not a large ship, being just 84ft long, but she was well armed with a dozen 6-pounder guns and a crew of seventy. Near the island of Malta, the *Enterprise* happened to encounter a corsair sailing from Tripoli called, appropriately enough, the *Tripoli*. For an account of what followed, we cannot do better than read a contemporary account from an American newspaper. On 18 November 1801, the Washington *National Intelligencer* reported that:

> Yesterday Captain Sterret, commander of the schooner Enterprize, part of the Mediterranean squadron, arrived here, with dispatches for the Secretary of the Navy. Captain Sterret is bearer of dispatches from commodore Dale, which exhibit a detailed account of the proceedings and situation of the Mediterranean squadron.
>
> On the 1st of August, the schooner Enterprize, commanded by Captain Sterret, and carrying 12 six pounders and 90 men, bound to Malta for a supply of water, fell in with a Tripolitan cruizer, being a ship of 14 six pounders, manned by 80 men. At this time the Enterprize bore British colours. Captain Sterret interrogated the commander of the Tripolitan on the object of his cruize. He replied that he came out to

cruise after the Americans, and that he lamented that he had not come alongside of some of them. Captain Sterret, on this reply, hoisted American, in the room of British colours; and discharged a volley of musquetry; which the Tripolitan returned by a partial broadside.—This was the commencement of a hard fought action, which commenced at 9 am and continued for three hours.

Three times, during the action, the Tripolitan attempted to board the Enterprize, and was as often repulsed with great slaughter, which was greatly increased by the effective aid afforded by the Marines. Three times, also, the Tripolitan struck her colours, and as often treacherously renewed the action, with the hope of disabling the crew of captain Sterret, which, as is usual, when the enemy struck her colours, came on deck, and exposed themselves, while they gave three cheers as a mark of victory.

When for the third time, this treacherous attack was made, captain Sterret gave orders to sink the Tripolitan, on which a scene of furious combat ensuded, until the enemy cried for mercy. Captain Sterret, listening to the voice of humanity, even after such perfidious conduct, ordered the captain either to come himself, or to send some of his officers on board the Enterprize. He was informed that the boat of the Tripolitan was so shattered as to be unfit for use. He asked, what security there was, that if he should send his men in his own boat, they would not be murdered?

After numerous supplications & protestations the boat was sent: The crew of the Tripolitan was discovered to be in the most deplorable state. Out of eighty men, 20 were killed, and 30 wounded. Among the killed were the second lieutenant and Surgeon; and among the wounded were the Captain and first lieutenant. And so decisive was the fire of the Enterprize that the Tripolitan was found to be in a most perilous condition, having received 18 shot between wind and water.

When we compare this great slaughter, with the fact that not a single individual of the crew of the Enterprize was in the least degree injured, we are lost in surprise at the uncommon good fortune which accompanied our seamen, and at the superior management of Captain Sterrett. All the officers and sailors manifested the truest spirit, and sustained the greatest efforts during the engagement. All, therefore, are entitled to encomium for their valour and good conduct. The marines, especially, owing to the nearness of the vessels, which were within pistol shot of each other, were eminently useful.

After administering to the relief of the distresses of the wounded Tripolitans, and the wants of the crew, Capt. Sterrett ordered the ship of the enemy to be completely dismantled. Her masts were accordingly all cut down, and her guns thrown overboard. A spar was raised, on which was fixed, as a flag, a tattered sail; and in this condition the ship was dismissed.

On the arrival of the Tripolitan ship at Tripoli, so strong was the sensations of shame and indignation excited there, that the Bey ordered the wounded captain to be mounted on a Jack Ass, and paraded thro' the streets as an object of public scorn. After which he received 500 bastinadoes. So thunderstruck were the Tripolitans at this event, and at the apprehended destruction of their whole marine force, that the sailors, then employed at Tripoli on board of cruisers that were fitting out by the government, all deserted them, and not a man could be procured to navigate them.

The echoes of this action reverberate down to this day and we can see in the decisive naval action a foreshadowing of the role America plays today as the self-appointed guardians of the world order. The sending of frigates and schooners across the Atlantic, less than 20 years after the United States had become an independent nation, was to be the first of many such actions, which continue to this day. If an American president despatches an aircraft carrier to some troubled region today, he is following a tradition begun during what was to become known as the First Barbary War.

The oldest of American military songs commemorates the events in North Africa at that time and a few years later in 1803 and 1805. As we shall see, in 1805, United States marines were landed in Libya and took part in a small war. The newspaper article above explains too that the USS *Enterprise* also carried a contingent of marines and the first verse of the Hymn of the United States Marines, reads;

> From the Halls of Montezuma
> To the shores of Tripoli;
> We fight our country's battles
> On the land as on the sea;
> First to fight for right and freedom
> And to keep our honor clean;
> We are proud to claim the title
> Of United States Marine.

The resolute action of the United States at the beginning of the nineteenth century reminds one of differing attitudes towards hijackers and hostage-takers in the late twentieth century. Then too, there were some countries who favoured handing over ransom for their citizens when they were captured and held hostage, while there were others who adopted from the first as their motto, 'Millions for defence, but not one cent for tribute!' There are many parallels between the hijacking of airliners in the 1970s and the seizure of ships at sea 200 years earlier. Indeed, the similarities are positively uncanny. During the 1960s and 1970s Arab militants fighting for the destruction of Israel and establishment of an independent nation of Palestine in its place embarked upon a series of attacks which frequently entailed the seizure of aircraft belonging to Western countries such as Britain and Germany. For over a decade, hijacking and the subsequent demands made to governments became a regular feature in newspaper headlines. Just as with the Barbary corsairs, the individuals undertaking these acts were being sheltered and supported by sovereign nations. The usual response to such criminal activity, at least on the part of European governments, might almost have been designed to encourage further hijackings. One or two specific examples will illustrate the similarities between the hijackings of the 1970s and the taking of hostages for ransom by corsairs operating out of North Africa a few centuries earlier. They also show the wisdom of the newly-formed United States government when faced by demands for money which were accompanied by threats of violence.

On Tuesday, 22 February 1972, a Lufthansa flight from Delhi to Athens was hijacked by five men armed with guns and explosives. They were acting on behalf of the Popular Front for the Liberation of Palestine. There were 172 passengers on the aircraft and the crew were ordered to divert the flight to South Yemen, a desert country on the edge of the Arabian Peninsula. Once the plane had landed, a demand was made to the West German government for a ransom of US$5 million for the safe return of the aeroplane and all the passengers. Lufthansa was at that time the state airline of West Germany. The government of the Federal Republic immediately agreed to the demands of the hijackers and arranged for the ransom to be handed over in Beirut, following which the aeroplane passengers and crew were all released and those responsible for seizing the plane were taken into custody by the authorities in South Yemen. They were later released without charge, allegedly because South Yemen was given a million dollars of the ransom (Newton, 2002).

The way that the above incident took place, with the willing connivance of a government which shared in the profits of the whole affair, will perhaps remind readers of the situation in the Barbary States, where apparently independent bands of corsairs extracted ransom, which they shared with the government of whichever territory they were operating in.

Some countries refused to play these games; most notably the State of Israel. In 1970 an El Al flight from Amsterdam to New York was hijacked. The pilot put the plane into a steep dive, throwing the hijackers off balance, whereupon one was shot dead by a sky marshal and the other disarmed and arrested. Israeli policy was never to negotiate with anybody attempting to take hostages in order to make demands. Although those planning to seize hostages for ransom or other reasons thereafter gave the Israeli airline a wide berth, attempts were made from time to time to target Israelis and Jews travelling by other airlines. In 1976 a group of four men, some from the Popular Front for the Liberation of Palestine and others from a German terrorist group, took control of a French airliner flying from Tel Aviv to Paris. There were many Israelis and Jews on board and the plane was flown to Uganda, whose president, Idi Amin, was a Muslim who supported the operation. On arrival at Entebbe airport near Kampala, he welcomed the hijackers as friends. The demand was made for the release of imprisoned terrorists in Israel, but rather than bargain with those making the demand, Israel flew a team of commandos 2,500 miles and rescued the hostages, killing all the hijackers in the process, along with many Ugandan soldiers.

The year after the raid on Entebbe, another German plane belonging to Lufthansa was hijacked, again by a mixed group of Palestinians and German revolutionaries. When, after landing at various airports and being denied permission to land at other places, the aircraft touched down in Mogadishu, the capital of Somalia, the Germans were determined not to give in to any of the demands being made. Instead, just as the Israelis had done, West Germany flew commandos to Mogadishu, stormed the plane, killed the hijackers and rescued the hostages. It was actions such as those at Entebbe and Mogadishu which put an end to the enthusiasm for hijacking. Those staging such crimes did not in general have a death-wish and it was becoming clear that nobody was prepared any longer to negotiate.

The American naval assault on Tripoli in 1801 is very similar in many ways to the Israeli attack on the Ugandan airport in 1976. In both cases, the rulers of a nation were colluding with kidnappers and on both occasions, those doing so got their fingers badly burned when the military forces of another country refused to give in to threats, but rather responded with firm and prompt action. In both cases too, both the hijackers and the country sheltering them must have thought that the great distance between them and the country whose aeroplane or ship they had seized would serve to protect them from retaliation.

The attack on Tripoli in 1801 marked the beginning of what are sometimes known as the Barbary Wars. Left to their own devices, European powers like England and France would probably have been content to allow matters to drift on as they had been doing for many decades, paying annual sums of money to the rulers of the Ottoman provinces in return for a quiet life. The impetus for what happened over the next few years came entirely from the vigorous young country of the United States, which was not a part of Europe and was not minded to play by the same rules as everybody else. Having made their displeasure clear in 1801, the Americans repeated the lesson twice more, culminating in the events of 1805 (Bradford, 2006).

Although there were still many slaves in North Africa and the rest of the Ottoman Empire, the taking of European or American captives had turned into less of a slave trade and more of a commercial enterprise, with the expectation that the end result would be the freeing of the prisoners in exchange for large sums of money. Although the men taken from various ships were nominally enslaved, at least until their ransom was paid, it was in nobody's interest for them to be cruelly mistreated. They would certainly have to work for their keep until the money was handed over, but these men were in no danger of being castrated or sent to the galleys.

The days of the Barbary corsairs were coming to an end for other reasons, quite apart from the unwillingness of the Americans to be used as a cash-cow. None of the European powers had previously seen any particular point in colonizing North Africa. There were few resources of any kind and the natives were heavily armed and hostile. Times were changing though and establishing a foothold in that part of the world might be of sound, strategic importance in the not-too-distant future. Countries like Egypt and Algeria might not be of much economic use in themselves, but they could serve as springboards, providing access to other and more interesting regions. Egypt was a case in point.

Egypt was a part of the Ottoman Empire at the beginning of the nineteenth century. In 1798, during France's war with England, Napoleon Bonaparte was in Egypt and while there saw the remains of an ancient waterway which looked as though it might at one time have served to connect part of the Nile with the Red Sea. At that time, travelling to India and the Far East from Europe entailed sailing what was known as the Cape Route; that is to say down through the Atlantic Ocean to South Africa, rounding the Cape of Good Hope and then heading north through the Indian Ocean. This was a long and trying voyage, through seas which could be exceedingly rough and unpredictable. After returning to France, Napoleon considered the possibility of constructing a canal which would connect the Mediterranean Sea with the Red Sea and, from there, to the Indian Ocean. He abandoned this tentative scheme when surveyors reported that the surface of the Mediterranean was 33ft below that of the Red Sea. This would have meant that any canal would need a series of complicated and expensive locks, rendering its construction economically unviable.

It is worth remarking, by the by, that Napoleon's invasion of Egypt, which was a province of the Ottoman Empire, brought to an end the Mamluk dynasty which had ruled the country for centuries. The Mamluks were, as will be remembered, a caste of slave-warriors, many of whom were the descendants of European slaves.

As the era of the great European empires gathered pace, Egypt looked interesting to the English, who were in the process of taking control of India via their proxy, the East India Company. Travelling to and from India via the Cape Route was very time consuming. A short-cut through Egypt to the Red Sea would be a most attractive prospect and by the end of the nineteenth century the canal had been built and Egypt was a British Protectorate, more or less part of the empire. The French had their eyes on another Ottoman province, that of Algiers. At a time when Africa was on the verge of being divided up by those anxious to exploit its resources, the French did not wish to be left behind. Although Algiers and the area around it had little to recommend it, there was agricultural land and this could be farmed in a modern and scientific way by European settlers. The Spanish, for their part, already had bases in Morocco and were considering whether it might be worth taking over the entire country. In short, the Barbary Wars precipitated by the United States had the effect of firing the starting gun for something of a colonial land-race in North Africa. From being the scourge of the Mediterranean and preying upon European shipping, places like Algiers and Tunis were soon to become the prey of countries vastly more sophisticated than they themselves, countries with nascent empires and modern armies.

The First Barbary War ended in 1805 with another American assault on Tripoli, this time from both land and sea. The Bashaw of Tripoli, Yusuf Qaramanli, had twice been defeated by American naval squadrons, but was still technically at war with the United States when another force was despatched in 1803. This was commanded by Edward Preble. This expedition began disastrously when the frigate *Philadelphia* ran aground in shallow water near Tripoli harbour. It was quickly overrun by fighters from the city and the crew taken ashore to be used as bargaining chips. Notwithstanding this inauspicious start to his campaign, Captain Preble soon fought back, sending a party of men to burn the *Philadelphia*, so that it could not be used by the enemy, and then shelling Tripoli itself. He also arranged for his men to board, capture and sink a number of Tripolitanian gunboats.

Despite all the efforts of the American warships, it proved impossible to deliver a decisive blow against Tripoli and as the year 1804 continued, it seemed that the ruler of Tripoli was likely to win by default. All he had to do was sit tight and wait for the Americans to give up and sail back across the Atlantic. It was clear to Thomas Jefferson in Washington that some other means would be needed to break the deadlock. The former American consul to Tunis, a man called William Eaton who had once held the rank of captain in the United States army, was sent to North Africa as the 'Naval Agent to the Barbary States'. His brief was simple. He had to find a way of bringing the Bashaw of Tripoli to heel.

There can be little doubt that Eaton had a very exaggerated sense of his own importance, because no sooner had he arrived in the Mediterranean than he began styling himself 'General', a considerable rise in rank for a man who had only ever been a captain. At other times, he signed his letters 'Commander in Chief'. The reality was that William Eaton was really no more than a secret agent, who was supposed to be investigating cunning and underhand means of removing the Bashaw. It seemed to Eaton that the best way of achieving the desired end would be to organize an army and march on Tripoli (Lambert, 2007).

The plan devised by the 'Naval Agent to the Barbary States' was an audacious one. He found that the current Bashaw of Tripoli had a brother living in Egypt, a man called Hamet Qaramanli whose claim to the throne of Tripoli was stronger than that of the actual ruler. If this claimant could be installed as Bashaw by America, he would presumably be so grateful that he would at once promise to stop attacking ships belonging to the United States. William Eaton had seven United States marines at his disposal and the promise of support from American ships in the Mediterranean. He found Hamet Qaramanli living in Alexandria and offered to help him overthrow his brother. In effect, he gave the word of the American government that they would support Hamet Qaramanli if only he threw in his lot with them. Unsurprisingly, he agreed to this.

Having secured a legitimate rival claimant to the throne of Tripoli, William Eaton set about recruiting an army of mercenaries which, led by Eaton and his half-dozen marines, would march on Tripoli. The men he persuaded to sign up for his force were an ill-assorted collection of Greeks, Arabs and Berbers. Once he had gathered together 500 men, Eaton set off to march west across the desert to Tripoli. The first settlement of any size between 'General' Eaton's army and Tripoli itself was a town called Derna.

It took the better part of two months for Eaton's force to reach Derna. Various American ships were gathered off the coast, with the intention of helping him if he should meet any serious opposition. On the morning of 25 April 1805, William Eaton sent a message to the Governor of Derna, asking for permission to pass through his town and replenish his provisions for his army of mercenaries. It can hardly be supposed that he seriously expected the local Bey to accede to such a request and indeed the answer which he received was terse and to the point, 'Your head or mine'. The battle which followed is famous as being the first engagement fought on land by the United States outside its own continent.

With the assistance of a bombardment from the ships anchored offshore, Eaton was able to take Derna and find enough food and water for his men to allow them to prepare for the next stage of the journey, the assault on Tripoli. The Bashaw though was no fool and realized when he heard that Derna had fallen that his own city was at risk. He sued for peace and was offered very favourable terms, considering all that had passed. He undertook not to attack any more American ships and to free all the American slaves in Tripoli. For their part, America agreed to pay $60,000 as ransom for the men being freed. Article 2 of the treaty, signed on 10 June 1805, reads;

> The Bashaw of Tripoli shall deliver up to the American squadron now off Tripoli, all the Americans in his possession; and all the subjects of the Bashaw of Tripoli now in the power of the United States of America shall be delivered up to him; and as the number of Americans in possession of the Bashaw of Tripoli amounts to three hundred persons, more or less; and the number of Tripolino subjects in the power of the Americans to about, one hundred more or less; The Bashaw of Tripoli shall receive from the United States of America, the sum of sixty thousand dollars, as a payment for the difference between the prisoners herein mentioned.

As may be seen, the Americans agreed at the same time to release all the prisoners that they held. As for Hamet Qaramanli, the man whom the United States had promised to install on the throne of Tripoli, he had now served his purpose and was dropped like the proverbial hot potato. William Eaton was horrified and disgusted that his pledged word was now rendered worthless and he remained bitter for the rest of his life about what he saw as a dreadful betrayal of an ally. There are those today who see in the treatment of Hamet Qaramanli a foreshadowing of the way that America has treated subsequent supposed friends, when once they have outlived their usefulness. In October 2019 the *Wall Street Journal* carried an article about America's apparent inability to extricate itself from the Middle East and mentioned in passing that;

> America's involvement in the greater Middle East dates back to the country's earliest days—and also began with casting aside an ally. (*Wall Street Journal*, 2019)

Although France and England were themselves at war when the United States Navy began operating in Europe's backyard, as one might say, both nations could see that the writing was on the wall for any existing arrangements or accommodations with the Barbary States. The news that American troops had landed in North Africa and were undertaking military operations there focused the mind of the European powers wonderfully. Paying tribute to keep the corsairs at bay had worked well enough for a century or so and had also served to maintain a trading monopoly for the more powerful countries such as England and France, but times were changing and if anybody's soldiers were to be invading or occupying Algiers, Tripoli or Tunis, then it would be better if they were troops from one of the older countries of Europe, rather than some new nation on the other side of the world.

There was another complication at the time when the Americans were fighting the Barbary Wars in the Mediterranean and that was that for part of the time, the United States was also at war with England. This too was connected with privateering of a kind and sometimes downright piracy. During the Napoleonic Wars, both England and France attempted to blockade each other's country, with the intention of inflicting economic harm and perhaps causing hardships to the ordinary citizens. The aim was to try and reach a situation where the enemy's population was starving or, at the very least, going short of various commodities. The British blockade was aimed at preventing any neutral nation, including the United States, from trading with France. This in turn led to a very strange situation whereby Britain herself, which had for long been condemning the Barbary corsairs for taking their sailors prisoner and making slaves of them did something almost identical themselves, which led in 1812 to a state of war between Britain and the United States.

As we have seen, corsairs or privateers sailing from ports on the Barbary Coast were in the habit of stopping ships belonging to European countries or the United States and seizing the crew as slaves. For a time, many of the sailors captured in this way would end up as crew members on galleys, being condemned to row naval vessels belonging to the navies of Tripoli, Algiers or Tunis. The British, in particular, grew very angry at this sort of thing and regarded it as an absolute outrage that sailors on the high sea could be kidnapped in this way and forced to help the navy of an enemy. This makes it all the stranger that the British should themselves use such tactics against other countries with whom they were not in a state of war. It will hardly come as a surprise to discover that it all ended in provoking a full-scale war.

Most people have heard of the press gangs which used to roam English seaports in the late eighteenth and early nineteenth centuries. During time of war, it was impossible to find enough volunteers to join the Royal Navy and so an early form of conscription was devised, whereby experienced sailors from merchant ships were forcibly transferred to the warships of the navy. A government department called the Impress Service oversaw this process. During the Napoleonic Wars, the Royal Navy greatly increased in size and required over 100,000 new recruits to man the vessels which were being built. There simply were not enough merchant seamen to go around and so the Impress Service authorized the Royal Navy to take any able-bodied man upon whom they could lay their hands. This was achieved by sending parties of sturdy sailors around the streets of ports at night and grabbing any likely fellow and bundling him aboard their ship. Although this sounds like a shocking way for the government to carry on, it was really no more than a primitive and rough-and-ready form of the conscription which was enforced in Britain during the First and Second World Wars.

Merchant seamen were certainly more use on a ship than some random farm labourer and there was a ready supply of such men to be had, although not in Britain itself. This was connected with another problem which Britain was tackling in the early years of the nineteenth century, which was to prevent America trading with France and to ensure that the cotton and tobacco being produced in the United States continued to be brought across the Atlantic to this country. Despite the American War of Independence fought against Britain, over 80 per cent of the cotton produced in the United States was exported to Britain at this time. Around 50 per cent of America's other exports were also made to Britain. The solution to both of these perceived difficulties was answered from 1807 onwards by the Royal Navy stationing ships around America ports and setting a watch on the vessels coming and going. This ensured that no French merchant ships were able to carry goods away from America. Being subjected to what looked increasingly like a blockade was infuriating enough for the United States, but there was worse to come.

Many members of the crews of American ships had not been born in the United States but were recent immigrants. In some cases, these men were deserters from the Royal Navy. As far as Britain was concerned, they had every right to stop and search ships, removing from them anybody born in Britain and enlisting them against their will in the Royal Navy. After all, this was the procedure commonly used in Britain itself; why should it not also be applied to British men on the high seas? One of the earliest such actions took place in 1807 and became known as the *Chesapeake–Leopard* affair.

On 22 June 1807 the American frigate *Chesapeake*, sailing from Virginia, was intercepted by a British warship, HMS *Leopard*. The captain of the *Leopard* had been ordered to search the American vessel for any deserters from the Royal Navy. Being unwilling to submit to what he regarded as an act of piracy, the commander of the *Chesapeake*, Commodore James Barron, declined to cooperate, whereupon the British opened fire, killing three men and wounding eighteen others, including Barron himself. At this point, the Americans surrendered and a boarding party took from their ship four men who had earlier been serving with the Royal Navy (Toll, 2006). One of these men was subsequently hanged after being court-martialled for desertion in time of war. The *Chesapeake–Leopard* affair created huge resentment in America and led five years later to a war with Britain. Illustration 17 is of Commodore Barron offering his sword as a token of surrender to a boarding party from the *Leopard*.

This diversion to examine Britain's relations with, and behaviour towards, the United States, has been undertaken to point out that the Royal Navy was carrying on in precisely the same way as the Barbary corsairs, whose conduct they had frequently condemned. Stopping ships at sea and taking men from them to crew your own warships was what the corsairs and their patrons had been at for many years. The war in 1812 between Britain and the United States was precipitated by much the same behaviour and when it ended, the British began once again encouraging the Barbary States to attack American shipping in the Mediterranean. They had done this 30 years or so earlier, after the British defeat during the American War of Independence, but America was a lot stronger now and had no intention of allowing the Algerians or any other country in the region to disrupt their trade with Europe. After attacks on their shipping in the Mediterranean, the United States did not hesitate to launch another expedition to punish the states whom they held responsible.

On 3 March 1815 a considerable naval force set sail from America and headed across the Atlantic. The ten ships, under the command of Commodore Stephen Decatur, had orders to proceed to Algiers and to deliver an ultimatum to the Dey (Allen, 1905). Almost as soon as they passed the Straits of Gibraltar and entered the Mediterranean, the American squadron encountered the Algerian flagship *Meshuda*, which they captured following a brief fight. Before reaching the waters off the coast of Algiers, another Algerian ship was also taken.

The Dey of Algiers was presented with a simple and stark choice. He could either release all American slaves being held in his country and pay compensation for the damage previously done to American shipping or the Americans would reduce Algiers to rubble. It was not very hard for the Dey to make a decision and on 3 July he signed a treaty in which he agreed to free all Americans, pay $10,000 compensation and guarantee never to trouble American shipping in the future. In return, Commodore Decatur returned the two ships he had captured, along with 500 or so men who had crewed them (Leiner, 2007). This ended the so-called Second Barbary War, with America showing Europe how states such as Algiers and Tripoli should be dealt with. Perhaps spurred on by the example of America, the British launched their own action against Algiers the following year.

There were still many European slaves in North Africa, although the corsairs had avoided taking men from powerful countries, restricting themselves in the main to fishermen from Mediterranean islands such as Corsica. The chaos of the Napoleonic Wars had rather distracted attention from the problem of the Barbary States, but after the Battle of Waterloo brought the wars against France to an end for good, the attention of Britain and one or two other countries turned to the Mediterranean and it was decided that determined action should be taken to bring an end to the problem caused by the petty rulers of the Barbary provinces. Although British ships had been left unmolested since the tribute system had been established, fishing boats from smaller nations had continued to be intercepted at sea and the crews taken off and sold as slaves. The British felt that following the decisive victory over Napoleon, it was absurd that the Dey of Algiers should still be doing much as he pleased with Christians from Sicily, Sardinia and other islands in the region.

Early in 1816, with Europe at peace and no other military distractions, Britain sent a diplomatic mission, led by Admiral Edward Pellew and backed by a squadron of warships, to the Dey of Algiers and the rulers of Tunis and Tripoli. The demands were simple and eminently reasonable. All Christian slaves were to be freed and there was to be no more piracy or corsair activity in the Mediterranean. Seeing clearly which way the wind was blowing, especially after the American show of force in 1815, the rulers of Tripoli and Tunis agreed at once and without quibbling to do as the British wished (Taylor, 2012). The Algerians proved recalcitrant, however, and were not at all disposed to agree to the British terms. Eventually though, they too agreed to what was being asked of them and Admiral Pellew, who was also Viscount Exmouth, returned to Britain, believing that he had achieved all that he had set out to do. No sooner had he left the Mediterranean though, than the Dey of Algiers, who had felt humiliated by the threats of the British, found a way to assuage his wounded pride. His troops massacred hundreds of Corsican, Sicilian and Sardinian slaves, fishermen who had been snatched from their boats and brought to Africa.

When news of the outrage reached Britain, Admiral Pellew was ordered to set sail at once and return to Algiers. According to the agreement which he had reached, all the Christian slaves in Algiers were under British protection and by having them killed in cold blood, the Dey had violated in the grossest way possible the treaty to which he had pledged his word. When the squadron of the Royal Navy anchored near Algiers this time, the negotiations were much briefer. Not only was there a British fleet, the Dutch had also a bone to pick with the Algerians, having had ships of their own taken by corsairs, and six of their ships had accompanied Admiral Pellew on his second mission.

In retrospect, it is plain that the days of the Barbary corsairs were over. With the coming of the Industrial Revolution and the swiftly-gathering pace of European colonialism it was a strange anachronism that the activities of these little provinces or states had not already been brought under control. Whatever the reason, by 1816 it was grotesque that a small province of the declining Ottoman Empire could be allowed the pretension of being on equal terms with the great European powers. This was not however as matters presented themselves to the Dey of Algiers and when the combined British and Dutch naval force arrived, he was in no mood for bargaining. The terms offered were reasonable enough; the immediate release of all European slaves and a permanent end to the predations of the corsairs sailing from Algiers. The Dey refused, expecting to be able to haggle for conditions a little more to his advantage. It was a serious miscalculation on his part.

The day following the delivery to the Dey of the British demands, it was clear that there was going to be fighting. Both sides had claimed that they would not fire the first shot, but the Dey had plans for sending parties of troops in small boats to board and, it was hoped capture, the ships of the Royal Navy which were laying at anchor in the bay in front of Algiers. For their part, the British were also planning to land troops on shore and assault the city from the land. At 3:15pm though, all these plans were wrecked when a trigger-happy Algerian on board one of the flotilla of small boats which were heading towards the British and Dutch fleet opened fire prematurely. It was sufficient excuse for Viscount Exmouth to begin a ferocious bombardment, not only of the approaching Algerian vessels, but also of the city itself.

The Algerians had shore batteries and also some mortars, but they were vastly outgunned by the Europeans. The battle which followed was costly on both sides. The British ships were equipped not only with mortars, which fired explosive shells in high arcs, landing almost vertically upon enemy positions, but also had a good stock of unguided rockets. These were notoriously inaccurate, but when fired randomly against a city were sure to cause damage to the enemy. The chief weapon of the attacking ships was of course the ordinary cannons, firing solid, metal balls which are technically known as round shot. Over a period of nine hours, 50,000 of these were discharged at Algiers and the Algerian ships which were attempting to attack the British squadron.

Although the final result was never really in doubt, the Algerians managed to inflict considerable casualties on the British. The next morning it was discovered that 128 men had been killed on the British side and another 700 or so wounded. This was a casualty rate of 16 per cent killed or wounded, which compared unfavourably with the figures at the Battle of Trafalgar, a decade earlier, when the rate had been just 9 per cent. Illustration 18 shows some of the fierce hand-to-hand fighting which took place that day, while Illustration 19 is of the bombardment itself. The object of the enterprise had been achieved, despite the heavy British casualties, in that the Algerian fleet was in ruins and the gun emplacements on shore destroyed. What the British commander knew, but the Algerians mercifully did not, was that almost all their ammunition had been expended in the engagement. Those 50,000 cannonballs had been propelled by 118 tons of gunpowder and the British squadron was in no position at all to continue the action. So ruinous though had the bombardment been for the Algerians that Viscount Exmouth thought it worth trying to bluff the Dey. On 28 August, he sent the following message;

> Sir, for your atrocities at Bona on defenceless Christians, and your unbecoming disregard of the demands I made yesterday in the name of the Prince Regent of England, the fleet under my orders has given you a signal chastisement, by the total destruction of your navy, storehouse, and arsenal, with half your batteries. As England does not war for the destruction of cities, I am unwilling to visit your personal cruelties upon the unoffending inhabitants of the country, and I therefore offer you the same terms of peace which I conveyed to you yesterday in my Sovereign's name. Without the acceptance of these terms, you can have no peace with England.

Unsurprisingly, the Dey of Algiers felt it wise to accept the terms which he had rejected less than 48 hours earlier. Over 1,000 slaves were freed and the British consul and his family, who had been in an invidious situation, was taken aboard one of the British ships. The Dey also agreed to refund all the ransom which he had so far received that year, which amounted to £80,000, a vast sum of money in those days. Some British officers went ashore to see for themselves the conditions under which the slaves were held. One such man was Captain Croker and

Illustration 20 is of some contemporary drawings which were based on information provided by Croker.

With the bombardment of Algiers in 1816, Europe's difficulties with the Barbary provinces of the Ottoman Empire more or less came to a close. The after-effects though, lingered on well into the twentieth century and were pivotal in French political affairs as late as the 1960s. It is no exaggeration to say that the long-term consequences of the Barbary corsairs and their actions came very near to causing a civil war in France just 60 years ago. More recently, the after-effects of the trade in white slaves nearly caused Britain and America to go to war with Russia as late as 1999. We shall explore these subjects in the final chapter.

Chapter 12

The Aftershock

The final end of the Barbary corsairs and their habit of capturing Europeans and Americans as slaves did not of course mean the end of Arab involvement in the slave trade. It is an iron rule of economics that so long as there is a demand for some product or service, there will be people who undertake to provide it. Any law limiting or prohibiting the provision of any service or the supply of goods will be ignored, providing of course that the prospective profits are sufficiently large. This applies today to such things as illegal drugs and it was the case during the nineteenth century, when slavery was frowned upon and discouraged by Britain and many other countries. There was a demand for slaves in Arab countries and if they could not be taken from Europe then they could be found elsewhere. The market for slaves was not limited to Arab countries, of course. There were others who were keen to buy them.

It is sometimes forgotten that the United States abolished its own trade in slaves in 1798, just a year after Britain passed a law outlawing the slave trade in the British Empire. Neither law had the effect of freeing slaves and the institution of slavery lingered on for years after the abolition of buying and selling human beings, particularly in the United States, where slavery was still going strong in the 1860s. It is worth bearing in mind too, that laws passed in Britain and America had little effect on the slave trade in Africa, which continued much as it had been doing for many centuries. The number of black Africans being murdered or enslaved by people from outside their continent did not diminish and the nineteenth century saw a rise in demand for slaves, a fact seldom mentioned in British and American history books.

Of course, human nature being what it is, there were those who sought to circumvent the law and continue to transport slaves across the Atlantic to both North and South America. Whaling ships were sometimes used for this purpose by slavers from America. By and large though, the transatlantic slave trade was over. The British navy patrolled the west coast of Africa to enforce the ban and it was obvious to most people that there would be no more large-scale transportation of slaves from Africa to the New World. The situation was very different on the other side of the African continent.

We have seen how the Arabs and Ottomans were enthusiastic about the use of slaves, many of whom came from Europe. They did not limit their attentions to the north though and at the same time that the Barbary Pirates were launching attacks on undefended stretches of coastline in Southern and Western Europe, black slaves were being acquired in Egypt, brought up the Nile from Sudan. There was a far more extensive trade south of Egypt and the Sudan though and this was worse both in the conditions and mortality rate than the Atlantic slave trade had ever been.

There had been, since at least the fourteenth century, a demand for African ivory, which is of course nothing more than the tusks of elephants. Before the advent of plastics, ivory was used for every imaginable purpose, from jewellery and combs to billiard balls and piano keys, to decorate musical instruments and make household goods. Wherever we now use synthetic plastics, at one time the tusks of elephants would have been used instead. This accounts in large measure for the low numbers of elephants in Africa today. The wonder of it is that there any left at all. There was certainly a great demand in Europe for this versatile substance, but the Arab nations too were very fond of ivory.

Neither Europeans nor Arabs of course initiated the export of ivory from Africa. The use of ivory was a byword for luxury as far back as the reign of Israel's King Solomon in around 1000 BC. Solomon used ivory to decorate his palace and sent far afield to acquire it;

For the king had at sea the ships of Tarshish with the ships of Hiram; once every three years the ships of Tarshish came bringing gold and silver, ivory and apes and peacocks. (1 Kings 10:22)

There was an insatiable desire for ivory, especially in the Arab world. One problem about moving elephant tusks hundreds of miles across Africa to the coast is that they are very heavy. The average tusk of an African elephant is something over two metres in length and weighs 23–45kg (or 51–99lbs). Imagine the logistics of transporting dozens or scores of such things over long distances. Labour would cost a fortune, unless of course one could have these heavy items carried all those miles for nothing. So it was that brilliant scheme was hit upon by the Arab traders on the east coast of Africa near the island of Zanzibar. If one could enslave a large number of healthy young men and then get them to carry those tusks, then it would be a case of killing two birds with one stone; ruinously high labour costs would be avoided and one would arrive at the coast with not one, but two valuable commodities; slaves and ivory. Both could then be sold.

The Arab slave trade which flourished in East Africa throughout the nineteenth century was at least as costly in suffering and the number of lives lost as the better-known transatlantic trade. Indeed, there is reason to suppose that far more lives were lost as a result of the slave raids and massacres carried out by the Arabs than was the case with the triangular trade. Suppressing the trade in white European slaves had the unintended effect of stimulating demand for black African slaves. As the Barbary corsairs declined towards the end of the eighteenth century, so the trade in Africans increased. After all, the Arabs had to get their slaves from somewhere, now that Europe was off limits. There was money to be made too from selling slaves for export to both North and South America. The British navy was patrolling the coast of West Africa in order to suppress the slave trade from what is now Ghana and Nigeria. Some American ships therefore sailed around the Cape of Good Hope and bought slaves from the east coast of Africa to take back to the United States. There was a demand for slaves in Brazil as well and traders from that country also came to Zanzibar and what is now Tanzania and Mozambique to buy their stock.

It is curious that with all the angst which Europeans are expected to suffer for the sins of colonialism in parts of the word such as Africa that nobody ever seems to recall the Arab colonialism which also resulted in the exploitation of Africa. The reason that Swahili, which used to be known a century ago as 'coast Arabic' and which was written in Arabic script, became the lingua franca of East Africa was because of the Arab slavers and colonists who settled in this part of Africa to see how much they could steal of the continent's natural resources, including the people living there. Zanzibar, the island which is now part of Tanzania, was a colony of Oman and the major centre for slavery in that part of the world during the nineteenth century. Slave caravans travelled from as far away as central Africa, bringing ivory and slaves to the coast. The conditions of these poor wretches who had been snatched from their homes were every bit as dreadful as those endured during the far better-known 'Middle Passage'. We read an account of an encounter with such slavers by David Livingstone in an earlier chapter, but it did not perhaps show with sufficient clarity what a terrible scourge the Arabs were on Africa at this time.

There was, as has already been remarked, a strong tradition of slavery in Africa long before either Arabs or Europeans set foot in the continent and both white Christians and Arab Muslims found no shortage of local men who would lend a hand in the capture and transportation of slaves. Together, they depopulated vast tracts of Africa. Here is a description written by a British traveller of the state of the country after the Arabs had been hunting for slaves;

> It was but yesterday that an explorer crossing from Lake Nyasa to Lake Tanganyika, saw the whole southern end of Tanganyika peopled with large and prosperous villages. The next to follow him found not a solitary human being – nothing but burned houses and bleaching skeletons. It was but yesterday – the close of 1887 – that the Arabs at the north end of Lake Nyasa, after destroying 14 villages with their inhabitants, pursued the population of one village into a patch of tall dry grass, set it on fire, surrounded it, and slew with the bullet and the spear those who crawled out from the more merciful flames.

Massacres of this kind, in the course of hunting for and capturing slaves, were common. It has been estimated that between 80,000 and 100,000 Africans died each year as a direct result of the Arab slave trade (Coupland, 1938). David Livingstone thought that ten times as many people died in this way. If so, then in the nineteenth century alone, well over 10 to 20 million people might have lost their lives in this way. Here is David Livingstone again, describing a slave caravan heading across Africa towards the Omani colony of Zanzibar in the 1870s;

> A more terrible sight than these men, women and children, I do not think I ever came across. To say that they were emaciated would not give you an idea of what human beings can undergo under certain circumstances . . . We went on further and were shown a place where a child lay. It had been recently born, and its mother was unable to carry it on from debility and exhaustion; so the slave trader had taken this little infant by its feet and dashed out its brains against one of the trees . . .

We have in this book looked at slavery as it has been practised in many countries. It was observed in the Introduction that there is a common feeling that people in Britain should feel exceptionally ashamed of their country's association with the slave trade and that this ties in with attempts to 'decolonize' the curricula of schools and universities. It is very interesting in this connection to examine the record of other countries and their own dealings with slavery and the slave trade. Just to remind readers, Britain and America led the world in abolishing the slave trade. Both countries made the importation of, or international trade in, slaves illegal in 1807. As soon as the Napoleonic Wars came to an end, Britain sent warships to West Africa to enforce this ban. The ownership of slaves lingered on in the British Empire until 1833 and in the United States for another 30 years after that. Since Britain is today constantly invited to feel guilty for taking so long to abandon the trade in and ownership of slaves, it is curious to see how long it took some other countries; countries which have escaped censure on these grounds.

We have looked in detail at the Ottoman Empire's involvement in the slave trade. This was not ended by law until 1908, a century after the British halted the practice. In Morocco, slavery was not abolished until 1922 and slaves in Kuwait had to wait until 1949 to be freed. Astonishingly, it was to be 1961 before Saudi Arabia reluctantly freed all the slaves in the country, but it was by no means the last country in the world to do so. We saw earlier in this chapter that Oman was very enthusiastic about slavery, especially in Zanzibar. It was 1970 when slavery was finally brought to an end there. There was still one country which showed a marked reluctance to put an end to slavery and the slave trade and this was the African country of Mauritania, a Muslim state. In 1976, they became the last country in the world to accept that slavery was morally wrong and to abolish it. One cannot help but wonder why there have never been demands for the Muslim countries who hung onto slavery and the slave trade for so much longer than Britain, to admit their own culpability and perhaps issue some kind of *mea culpa*. After all, their own prosperity was founded upon the slave trade every bit as much as was that of Britain.

The idea has been touched upon several times in this book that many situations and events in the modern world have their roots in the capture of white European slaves and their exploitation by Muslims in North Africa and the Middle East. America's continued involvement in the Middle East and regular attempts at what has become known as 'regime change' has often appeared in newspapers since the First Barbary War. This had become such a notable feature of American foreign policy that during the 2011 intervention in Libya, when America and other countries were attempting set up a democratic regime to replace that of the autocratic Colonel Gaddafi, some observers began referring to it as the Third Barbary War. The fact that almost 200 years after the failed attempt to install their puppet in Tripoli, the Americans were at it again was seen as an indication that they could never quite free themselves of the habit of interfering in the affairs of Middle Eastern nations.

The Americans have always acted through proxies in Africa and Asia, never pursuing a policy of naked colonialism but always disguising their intentions with the fig-leaf of democracy by supporting this or that leader whom they believe will act more in keeping with American aims and objectives than whoever is currently ruling the country. European countries in the nineteenth century were a little more direct about what they were up to. When France wished to expand outward from her borders into Africa, they did not bother with any complicated justifications, but seized the flimsiest of excuses and grabbed whatever territory it was to which they had taken a liking. This is what happened with Algiers.

After the bombardment of Algiers in 1816, it was obvious to the countries of Europe that the menace of the Barbary corsairs was over. This did not mean that there would be no further military dealings between Europe and North Africa though, far from it. Seeing the Dey of Algiers humbled and his once formidable power set at naught caused some people in Europe to think hard about what advantage a powerless and enfeebled area of North Africa might mean to their country. Colonies had already been established in many distant parts of the world; North and South America, the Caribbean, the Far East and so on. Here was territory in another continent which was right on Europe's doorstep and simply waiting for some enterprising country to occupy and civilize it.

Some Barbary corsairs still operated in the Mediterranean, even after the decisive British victory over Algiers, but these were more a nuisance than a threat. There was some bad blood between France which dated back to a dispute over some debts incurred during the time of the French Republic, at the end of the eighteenth century. The details need not concern us, but essentially the French owed Algiers money for goods supplied during the 1790s. Now that the monarchy had been restored, following the fall of Napoleon, the new king felt under no obligation to settle the debts of what he regarded as an illegal regime. This dispute flared up into open hostility in 1827, with what became known as the 'Fan Affair'. During a meeting between the Dey of Algiers and the French consul, the Dey had become so irritated at the French attitude that he had struck the consul lightly with a fly-whisk which he happened to be holding. No injury was caused, but the French government chose to interpret this as a matter of honour and instituted a naval blockade of Algiers.

We pause at this point to recall two points. The first is that the French had something of a grudge already against the Algerians, when it came to mistreating consuls! As we saw in an earlier chapter, two French consuls had met their deaths in Algiers after being blown from the mouth of a cannon. It is by no means impossible that this accounted, at least in part, for the over-reaction by France to the trifling blow from a fly-whisk received by another of their consuls. There was another reason though that matters escalated and that was that the Bourbon monarchy were not especially popular among ordinary people in France. It was said of the Bourbons that they had not learned the lessons which led to the revolution in France. After Charles X became king in 1824, Talleyrand remarked that the French royal family had 'learned nothing and forgotten nothing'. By 1830, revolution was once again in the air, as anybody who has read the book *Les Miserables*, or seen the musical or film based upon it, will know.

One tried and tested method for dealing with domestic unpopularity is of course to start a small and successful foreign war. This often has the effect of rousing latent patriotism and causing people to forget about such minor issues as unemployment and hunger. One recalls the way in which the fortunes of Margaret Thatcher's unpopular administration were dramatically transformed in 1982, by the recapture of the Falkland Islands. The election held the following year gave Thatcher an astonishing 144-seat majority. Charles X and his advisers followed a similar strategy in 1830. There was of course no election scheduled that year, but the French population appeared in the mood to replace their king in the same way that they had 40 years earlier.

After a lengthy blockade of Algiers, which caused more harm to French trade than it did to the Algerians, the Dey's guns opened fire on a French ship. It was enough to trigger a full-scale invasion of that part of North Africa. A huge armada of 600 ships transported an army of 34,000 soldiers to conquer Algiers and the surrounding territory. The campaign lasted just three weeks and ended in the surrender of the Dey and an orgy of looting and killing by the French troops as they took Algiers. Once settled there, they colonized both Algeria and also Tunis and the land around it which became the country of Tunisia.

Over the next 130 years Algeria came to hold the same status as France itself, that is to say that it was an integral part of the country. Algiers was as much French territory as Paris or Lyons. This led to the bizarre situation that when the European Economic Community was founded in 1958, it included almost 2.5 million square kilometres of Africa! Such a colonial anachronism could not last indefinitely and with increasing resistance to French rule from the indigenous inhabitants, a bitter war broke out, which threatened to engulf France itself. A military coup in Algeria led to the landing of paratroopers to seize Corsica and plans to take Paris in the same way. Civil war was averted by a hair's breadth, when Charles de Gaulle came out of retirement to lead the nation, but it had been a close-run thing. All this had its roots in the troubles with the Barbary States in the seventeenth century. It is no exaggeration to say that the death of Jean Le Vacher in 1683 had been the beginning of sequence of events which led to the appointment of Charles de Gaulle as president of France in the years following the end of the Second World War.

The founding of France's Fifth Republic under Charles de Gaulle in 1958 is one important political development since the Second World War which had its roots in the taking of slaves from Europe. The historical consequences of de Gaulle's accession to power were far-reaching, not least for Britain. It was of course Charles de Gaulle who was so bitterly opposed to the United Kingdom joining the European Union or Common Market, as it was then known. The relations which

Britain has had with the European Union, culminating in 2016 with the decision to leave, have been coloured by this early rejection.

Another and more recent example of the effects of the trade in white slaves and their use in Muslim countries was the first combat operation in the history of NATO, the North Atlantic Treaty Organization. This led eventually to the confrontation of Russia troops with those of NATO, a situation fraught with hazard and which General Mike Jackson of the British army said at the time could have led to what he called a 'Third World War'.

We have already looked a little at the ethnic conflicts which erupted in the 1990s in the territory of what used to be Yugoslavia. These simmered away for years and as fast as one died down, another arose. Both NATO and the United Nations were involved at different times. NATO had been founded in 1949 as an American-backed military counter-balance to the Russian forces in Eastern Europe. For 45 years, NATO managed to act as a deterrent to Russian expansion in Europe, without firing a single shot. Then troops from NATO took the role of peacekeepers in the war between Serbia, which claimed to be the legitimate authority in those regions which had once made up Yugoslavia. When a no-fly zone was declared over Bosnia, the Serbs ignored it and began bombing Bosnian positions. On 28 February 1994, NATO forces shot down four Serbian planes, the first shots ever fired in anger by the organization.

During the chaos of the disintegration of Yugoslavia, a province of Serbia called Kosovo took its chance and attempted to secede and form an independent nation. Nowhere could the legacy of the former Ottoman Empire and their activities in the Balkans be more clearly seen than in the ethnic and religious composition of Kosovo, as opposed to the rest of Serbia. Over 90 per cent of those living in Kosovo were Muslims, the majority of whom were Albanian. By contrast, in Serbia just 3 per cent of the population were Muslim. The Serbs are Slavs and because of the history at which we have looked, have little love for Muslims, by who they feel they were oppressed for centuries. The shadow cast by the devshirme, which principally took place in the Balkans, is a long one.

The Russians, essentially a Slav nation, have always seen themselves as the protectors and guarantors of Slav interests, especially in the Balkans. It was of course Russia's support of the Serbs in 1914 which helped to trigger the First World War. When they saw, as they thought, Serbs being pushed around in the Balkans in the 1990s, they acted to intervene on behalf of their fellow Slavs, sending their own peacekeepers, who acted independently of NATO and the United Nations. It was perhaps inevitable that this would sooner or later lead to trouble.

Serbia had no intention of giving up one of its provinces without a fight. Since it was the Albanian Muslims who were behind the move to secede, Serbia, under its leader Slobodan Milosevic, thought that a better scheme would be to drive them from the province instead. To prevent this ethnic cleansing, NATO launched a bombing campaign against Belgrade. When the fighting ended in June 1999, it looked as though Kosovo might be allowed to exist separately from Serbia. This seemed to the Russians an affront to Slav pride and on the morning of 11 June, a column of Russian armoured vehicles drove from Bosnia to the Kosovan capital Pristina and seized the airport. It was suspected that they would then use the airport to fly in reinforcements of Russian troops and then work with Serbia to partition Kosovo into a Slav north and a Muslim south. This prospect would have meant that all NATO's eforts had been in vain.

The American General in charge of NATO operations in Kosovo was Wesley Clark, the Supreme Allied Commander Europe, and he was furious to see the Russians apparently preparing to help Serbia take over half the province and ordered his subordinate, British General Mike Jackson, to block the runway of Pristina airport with armoured vehicles, to prevent any Russian aircraft carrying reinforcements from landing. Jackson refused to obey this order, telling Clark, 'I'm not going to start the Third World War for you!' In the event, the Americans managed to bring pressure to bear on the governments of Romania, Bulgaria and Hungary, causing those countries to refuse permission for Russian aircraft to enter their airspace. It was perhaps the tensest moment in Europe since the fall of the Berlin Wall a decade earlier.

172 The Forgotten Slave Trade

These are just a few of the ways in which the Muslim desire for European slaves has caused shockwaves, the effects of which linger on to this very day. It is indeed strange that such a relatively unknown chapter in the history of the world could have had such a great influence upon lives today.

Endword

We have in this book traced the institution of slavery from ancient times, in various parts of the world, and found that it is the nearest thing to a universal custom or practice. Almost all cultures, on every continent, found the idea of human beings being owned and traded as commodities to be perfectly normal and acceptable. This was the case in Europe as in Africa, Asia as in the Americas. Slavery in Europe was found to be far more extensive and cruel than that associated with what we have now come to term 'the' slave trade; the transportation of black African slaves across the Atlantic Ocean to North America and the islands of the Caribbean. This leaves us with something of a conundrum or puzzle. Why is it that today any mention of slavery is automatically assumed to be a question of racial exploitation of black people by white Europeans or Americans?

Our modern perception of 'the' slave trade dates only from the 1960s and is a direct result of political changes and, in Britain, the large-scale arrival of immigrants from the Caribbean. The history taught in British schools until relatively recently, certainly up to the 1970s, dealt exclusively with the achievements of white men and women, the story of other ethnic groups and minorities being relegated to the sidelines. With increasing numbers of black children in schools, it was felt that their own history should also be included, lest they felt like outsiders or interlopers. This was a noble enough aim, but it has led to a skewing of our understanding of the past. Ensuring that Mary Seacole from Jamaica was mentioned alongside Florence Nightingale was harmless enough, if a little misleading. After all, Mary Seacole ran an hotel for officers, rather than working in a hospital. Portraying the enslavement of Africans by white people as the chief type of slavery in the world's history though has led many young white people to feel guilty and promoted a mentality of victimhood among a lot of black people.

In America, the case was rather different, because the black immigrants in that country did not arrive in the 1950s and 1960s but had been living there for over a century. It was not a physical arrival which took place, but a cultural one, as desegregation and the civil rights movement gradually took hold, at the same time that Britain was experiencing a great wave of newcomers from the New Commonwealth. The effect though was similar, in that black history became something which spread from being the preserve of a handful of enthusiasts to featuring in ordinary school classrooms. The Atlantic slave trade fitted neatly into this process, as it explained why so many people of African origin happened to be living in North America and the Caribbean.

There were no sinister or hidden motives on anybody's part in promoting the notion that the Atlantic slave trade was a dreadful thing and a matter of great injustice to its victims. All this was of course undeniably true. Nevertheless, with the growth of such things as Black History Month, which began in the United States in 1970 and arrived in Britain 17 years later, the transatlantic slave trade has become such a prominent part of the historical narrative in Britain and America, that it is hardly surprising that it has eclipsed and now replaced some of the history which had previously been taught. It is this which explains the 'cultural erasure' which has been referred to elsewhere in this book, the process whereby some of the events relating specifically to Europe's past have been overlooked and now largely forgotten. The idea of white British people as slaves in Africa is an example of this. In the introduction to this book, we saw that MP David Lammy was so familiar with the accepted narrative relating to slavery that when Ann Widdecombe talked of slaves overthrowing their owners, he was offended, because the only cases of such a thing that he could readily imagine were of black slaves and white owners. This mindset is, in Britain today, all but universal.

Without any intention of minimizing or disregarding the terrible experience of the Africans taken from their homes and transported thousands of miles to another continent, the aim of this book has been to show that this was not a uniquely horrible event and that Europe's history of enduring slavery is comparable to that of Africa. We saw that under the Roman Republic and Empire, many millions of Europeans were taken into slavery and that during the centuries which followed the decline of the Roman world, slavery continued to be practised across the continent, with Muslims in Africa playing a key role in the process. If this book serves only to redress the balance a little and bring the European experience of slavery back into sight, then its purpose will have been served.

References

Ágoston, Gábor (2014), 'Firearms and Military Adaptation: The Ottomans and the European Military Revolution, 1450–1800', *Journal of World History* 25: 113.

Allen, Gardner W. (1905), *Our Navy and the Barbary Corsairs*. Boston: Houghton Mifflin.

Anderson, R.C. (1952), *Naval Wars in the Levant 1559–1853*. Princeton: Princeton University Press.

Andrewes, Antony (1971), *Greek Society*. London: Pelican Books.

Armstrong, Karen (2006), *Muhammed: A Prophet For Our Time*. London: HarperCollins.

Ayalon, David (1999), *Eunuchs, Caliphs and Sultans: A Study in Power Relationships*. Jerusalem: Magnes Press.

Balfour, Patrick & Kinross, Baron (1977), *The Ottoman Centuries: The Rise and Fall of the Turkish Empire*. London: Perennial.

BBC News Report (2019), 'Ann Widdecombe's EU slavery remarks branded as "disgusting"', 4/7/19.

Bede, The Venerable, ed. D. Farmer (2003), *Ecclesiastical History of the English People: With Bede's Letter to Egbert and Cuthbert's Letter on the Death of Bede*. London: Penguin Books.

Besant, Walter (1903), *London in the Time of the Stuarts*. London: Adam and Charles Black.

Booth, Mary (1865), *Martin's History of France: The Age of Louis XIV*. London: Walker, Wise and Company.

Boyd, Julian P., Bryan, Mina & Hutter, Elizabeth, L. (eds) (1953), *The Papers of Thomas Jefferson*. Princeton: Princeton University Press.

Bradford, James (ed.) (2006), *International Encyclopaedia of Military History*. London: Routledge.

Braudel, Fernand (1949), *The Mediterranean and the Mediterranean World in the Age of Philp II.* New York: Harper & Row.

Bridge, Anthony (1988), *Suleiman the Magnificent: Scourge of Heaven.* New York: Hippocrene Books.

Briggs, Asa (1983), *A Social History of England.* New York: The Viking Press.

Brotton, Jerry (2017), *This Orient Isle: Elizabethan England and the Islamic World.* London: Penguin.

Brown, Michael J. (1970), *Itinerant Ambassador: The Life of Sir Thomas Roe.* Lexington: University Press of Kentucky.

Bruce, Duncan A. (1998), *The Mark of the Scots: Their Astonishing Contributions to History, Science, Democracy, Literature, and the Arts.* New York: Citadel Press.

Burton, Richard (trans.) (1885), *The Book of the Thousand Nights and a Night.* London: Kama Shastra Society.

Calendar of State Papers Colonial, America and West Indies: Volume 1, 1574-1660. (1860) London: Her Majesty's Stationery Office.

Castleden, Rodney (2005), *Events That Changed The World.* London: Time Warner Books.

Chernaik, Warren L. (1964), 'Waller's Panegyric to My Lord Protector and the Poetry of Praise', *Studies in English Literature, 1500-1900*, Vol. 4, No. 1, Winter 1964.

Chisholm, Hugh (ed.) (1911), *Encyclopaedia Britannica.* Cambridge: Cambridge University Press.

Clarke, Duncan (1999), *Slaves and Slavery.* Rochester: Grange Books.

Coe, Michael D. & Houston, Stephen (2015), *The Maya.* London: Thames & Hudson.

Cotterell, Arthur (ed.) (1980), *The Encyclopaedia of Ancient Civilizations.* New York: Mayflower Books.

Coupland, Reginald (1938), *East Africa and Its Invaders from the Earliest Times to the Death of Seyyid Said in 1856.* Oxford: The Clarendon Press.

Cunliffe, Barry (ed.). (2001), *The Penguin Atlas of British and Irish History.* London: Penguin Books.

Daily Mail (2014), 'Roman slaves are unearthed . . . still with their iron collars and shackles in place', 4/12/14.

Daily Telegraph (2017), 'Memory of Cornish coast dwellers kidnapped for slavery "culturally erased"', 30/12/17.

Daily Telegraph (2019), 'Ann Widdecombe compares EU to slave owners', 4/7/19.

Dalrymple, William (2004), *White Mughals: Love and Betrayal in Eighteenth-century India*. London: Harper Perennial.

D'Arms, John H. & Kopf, E. Christian (eds) (1980), *Seaborne Commerce of Ancient Rome: Studies in Archaeology and History*. Rome: American Academy in Rome.

Davis, David Brion (1970), *The Problem of Slavery in Western Culture*. London: Pelican Books.

Davis, Robert C. (2003), *Christian Slaves, Muslim Masters: White Slavery in the Mediterranean, The Barbary Coast, and Italy, 1500-1800*. London: Palgrave Macmillan.

Davison, Michael Worth (ed.) (1992), *Everyday Life Through the Ages*. London: Reader's Digest Association.

Defoe, Daniel (1719), *Robinson Crusoe*. London: William Taylor.

Drummond, Henry (1897), *Tropical Africa*. London: Hodder & Stoughton.

Ducat, Jean (1990), *Les Hilotes (Bulletin de correspondance hellénique)*. Athens: École Française d'Athènes.

Dudley, D.R. (ed.) (1969), *The Penguin Companion to Literature: Classical & Byzantine, Oriental & African Literature*. London: Penguin Books.

Eliot, Sir John (1881), *An Apology for Socrates and Negotium Posterorum*. London: Alexander B. Groshart.

Elleman, Bruce, Rosenberg, David & Forbes, Andrew (2010), *Piracy and Maritime Crime: Historical and Modern Case Studies*. Newport: Naval War College (US) Press.

Everett, Suzanne (1997), *History of Slavery*. London: Grange Books.

Feldman, Martha (2015), *The Castrato: Reflections on Natures and Kinds*. Oakland: University of California Press.

Firth, C.H. & Rait, R.S. (1911), *Acts and Ordinances of the Interregnum, 1642-1660*. London: His Majesty's Stationery Office.

Fisher, Sir Godfrey (1957), *Barbary Legend: War, Trade and Piracy in North Africa 1415-1830*. Oxford: Clarendon Press.

Fogel, Robert William & Engerman, Stanley L. (1974), *Time on the Cross: The Economics of American Negro Slavery*. New York: W.W. Norton.

Foulke, William Dudley (trans.) (1974), *History of the Lombards*. Philadelphia: University of Philadelphia Press.

Fremont-Barnes, Gregory (2006), *The Wars of the Barbary Pirates*. London: Osprey.

Gordon, Matthew (2001), *The Breaking of a Thousand Swords: A History of the Turkish Military of Samarra, A.H. 200–275/815–889 C.E.* New York: State University of New York Press.

Grant, Reg (2009), *Slavery*. London: Dorling Kindersley.

Guardian (2019), 'Police chiefs in row over definition of Islamophobia', 15/5/19.

Harper, J. (1972), 'Slaves and Freedmen in Imperial Rome', *The American Journal of Philology*, vol. 93, no. 2, 1972, pp. 341–2.

Haywood, John (2008), *The Great Migrations: From the Earliest Humans to the Age of Globalisation*. London: Quercus.

Hibbert, Christopher (ed.) (1970), *The Pen and the Sword*. London: George Weidenfeld & Nicolson.

Holroyd, John, Earl of Sheffield (1783), *Observations on the commerce of the American states with Europe and the West Indies: including the several articles of import and export, and on the tendency of a bill now depending in Parliament*. London: J. Debrett

Homer, trans. Martin Hammond (1987), *The Iliad*. London: Penguin Classics.

Hreinsson, Karl Smari & Nichols, Adam (trans.) (2016), *The Travels of Reverend Ólafur Egilsson (Reisubók Séra Ólafs Egilssonar): The story of the Barbary corsair raid on Iceland in 1627*. Washington: Catholic University of America Press.

Huntington, Samuel P. (1996), *The Clash of Civilizations and the Remaking of World Order*. New York: Simon & Schuster.

Independent (2019), 'Bristol University appoints black history professor to expose institution's links with slave trade', 30/10/19.

Jaques, Tony (2006), *Dictionary of Battles and Sieges: A Guide to 8500 Battles from Antiquity Through the Twenty-first Century.* High Wycombe: Greenwood Press.

Joyce, P.W. (1911), *The Wonders of Ireland.* Dublin: Longman Green.

Kennedy, Hugh (2016), *The Caliphate.* London: Pelican Books.

Kesselring, K.J. (2003), *Mercy and Authority in the Tudor State.* Cambridge: Cambridge University Press.

Kipling, Rudyard & Fletcher, C.R.L (1911), *A School History of England.* Oxford: Clarendon Press.

Lambert, Frank (2007), *The Barbary Wars: American Independence in the Atlantic World.* New York: Hill & Wang.

Lang, Sean (2003), *British History for Dummies.* London: John Wiley and Sons.

Leiner, Frederic C. (2007), *The End of Barbary Terror, America's 1815 War against the Pirates of North Africa.* Oxford: Oxford University Press.

MacDonald, George F. (1996), *Haida: Children of the Eagle.* Gatineau: Canadian Museum of History.

Matar, Nabil (1998), *Islam in Britain 1558-1685.* Cambridge: Cambridge University Press.

Meynard, Charles Barbier de (trans.) (1865), *Des routes et des Provinces.* Paris: Journal Asiatique.

Miers, Suzanne & Kopytoff, Igor (1977), *Slavery in Africa: Historical and Anthropological Perspectives.* Wisconsin: University of Wisconsin Press.

Milton, Giles (2005), *White Gold: The Extraordinary Story of Thomas Pellow and North Africa's One Million European Slaves.* London: John Murray.

Monaghan, Tom (2008), *The Slave Trade.* London: Evans Brothers.

Morgan, Kenneth (ed.) (1984), *The Oxford History of Britain.* Oxford: Oxford University Press.

National Intelligencer (1801).

Newton, Michael (2002), *The Encyclopedia of Kidnappings*. New York: Facts on File.

Northup, Solomon (1853), *Twelve Years a Slave*. Auburn: Derby and Miller.

Ødegaard, Torbjørn (2010), *Oppgjøret med røverstaten Algier 1769-72*. Horten: Marinemuseet.

O Domhnaill, Ronan Gearoid (2015), *Fado Fado: More Tales of Lesser-Known Irish History*. London: Matador.

Parker, Philip (2014), *The Northmen's Fury: A History of the Viking World*. London: Vintage.

Parker, Richard B. (2004), *Uncle Sam in Barbary*. Gainesville: University Press of Florida.

Peach, L. du Garde (1960), *David Livingstone*. Loughborough: Wills & Hepworth.

Pelteret, David A.E. (2001), *Slavery in Early Mediaeval England from the Reign of Alfred Until the Twelfth Century (Studies in Anglo-Saxon History)*. Martlesham: Boydell Press.

Pcnzcr, N.M. (2005), *The Harem: Inside the Grand Seraglio of the Turkish Sultans*. New York: Dover Publications.

Pepys, Samuel (1661), *The Diary of Samuel Pepys: Volume I - 1660*.

Pipes, Daniel (1981), *Slave Soldiers and Islam: The Genesis of a Military System*. New Haven: Yale University Press.

Plato, trans. H.D.P. Lee (2007), *The Republic*. London: Penguin Books.

Prowse, Tracy L., Henry P. Schwarcz, Peter Garnsey, Martin Knyf, Roberto Macchiarelli, and Luca Bondioli (2007), 'Isotopic evidence for age-related immigration to imperial Rome', *American Journal of Physical Anthropology*, 132 (4): 510–19.

Ridgeway, John (1890), *Folklore, Vol. 1 No. 1*. London: The Folklore Society.

Robinson, Andrew (2002), *Lost Languages*. Bath: The Bath Press.

Rodgers, N. (2007), *Ireland, Slavery and Anti-Slavery: 1612-1865*. London: Palgrave Macmillan.

Rodriguez, Junius P. (1997), *The Historical Encyclopedia of World Slavery*. Santa Barbara: ABC-CLIO.

Schoff, Wilfred Harvey (1912), *The Periplus of the Erythraean Sea: Travel and Trade in the Indian Ocean by a Merchant of the First Century*. London: Longmans, Green.

Seaver, George (1957), *David Livingstone, His Life and Letters*. London: Lutterworth Press.

Singh, Upinder (2009), *A History of Ancient and Early Medieval India: From the Stone Age to the 12th Century*. Harlow: Pearson Education.

Strabo (1923), *Geography*. Translated by Horace Leonard Jones and published by the Loeb Classical Library.

Sumner, Charles (1853), *White Slavery in the Barbary States*. Boston: John P. Jewett.

Swanson, Claude A. (ed.) (1939), *Naval Documents Related to the United States Wars with the Barbary Powers*. Washington D.C.: U.S. Government Printing Office.

Syed, Muzaffar Husain (2011), *A Concise History of Islam*. India: VIJ Books (India) Pty.

The News & Observer (2007), 'Congo's Pygmies live as slaves', 12/3/07.

Taylor, Stephen (2012), *Commander: The Life and Exploits of Britain's Greatest Frigate Captain*. London: Faber and Faber.

Thorlby, Anthony (ed.) (1969), *The Penguin Companion to Literature: European*. London: Penguin Books.

Toll, Ian, (2006), *Six Frigates: The Epic History of the Founding of the U.S. Navy*. New York: W.W. Norton.

Tracy, Larissa (ed.) (2013), *Castration and Culture in the Middle Ages*. Martlesham: D.S. Brewer.

Trevelyan, G.M. (1942), *History of England*. New York: Longmans, Green.

UN News (2019), 'Scourge of slavery still claims 40 million victims worldwide, "must serve as a wakeup call"', 9/9/19.

Wall Street Journal (2019), 'America Can't Escape the Middle East', 25/10/19.

Wettinger, Godfrey (2002), *Slavery in the Islands of Malta and Gozo: Ca. 1000-1812*. San Gwann: Publishers Enterprise Group.

Wharton, Francis (compiler) (1888), *The Revolutionary Diplomatic Correspondence of the United States.* Washington.

Whitford, David M. (2009), *The Curse of Ham in the Early Modern Era: The Bible and the Justifications for Slavery.* Farnham: Ashgate.

Williams, Brenda (2006), *Ancient Britain.* Andover: Jarrold Publishing.

Williams, Hywel (2006), *Days that Changed the World.* London: Quercus.

Wilson, Jean & Roehrborn, Claus (1999), 'Long-Term Consequences of Castration in Men: Lessons from the Skoptzy and the Eunuchs of the Chinese and Ottoman Courts', *The Journal of Clinical Endocrinology & Metabolism*, Vol. 84, Issue 12, 1 December 1999, pp. 4324–31.

Index